Adventures Walking on Water

Dorea E. Ross Arguelles

iUniverse, Inc.
Bloomington

Adventures Walking on Water

iUniverse books may be ordered through booksellers or by contacting:

iUniverse
1663 Liberty Drive
Bloomington, IN 47403
www.iuniverse.com
1-800-Authors (1-800-288-4677)

ISBN: 978-1-4759-8608-2 (sc)
ISBN: 978-1-4759-8610-5 (hc)
ISBN: 978-1-4759-8609-9 (e)

Library of Congress Control Number: 2013907042

Printed in the United States of America

iUniverse rev. date: 4/30/2013

Dedication

I am so grateful for my children and the gift they have been to me. They have taught me much about love and sacrifice.

They gave encouragement as I worked on this book and gave their two cents when I asked for advice.

Thank you, Josh, for working for hours on end on the book cover and for retaking all of the pictures and editing them for me. Oh yes, and thank you for answering the endless questions about how to work the computer. I would much rather create something with my hands.

You children have made the biggest impact on my life, and I thank God for each one of you.

Remember, "Who are you?"

Love, Mom

Quote: Love is a Decision

"Adventures Walking on Water is truly an inspiring life story of Faith, Hope, and Love. (1 Cor. 13:- the greatest of these is love).

The life adventures of Dorea, Dav and their children manifest the omnipresence of God sharing the cross and the crown, the agony and ecstasy that make us want to know and love God more intimately. It's my privilege to know the author personally."
—Rev. Francis A. Pouliot

Contents

Acknowledgments

I want to thank so many people for being in my life.

First, I am so grateful for my family and friends in Biloxi, Mississippi. I can't even express my gratitude for their love for us.

My church family and friends in Pensacola, Florida, loved our family in incredible ways. Too many to individually name, but I thank all the people who cared for us in a special way when my son was sick those two years.

The Brotherhood of Hope made a huge impact on my spiritual life after my husband's death. That led me to the People of Hope for ten years. I grew in my faith tremendously. Thank you, People of Hope.

Thank you, Mary, for spending many hours with me editing and reediting. You are a joy to work with.

I want to also thank my spiritual directors for their guidance and patience.

Auxiliary Bishop Martin D. Holly of Washington, D.C,

Rev. James Carroll of Warren, New Jersey

Rev. Francis A Pouliot of St. Paul Minnesota

God bless you all.

The ultimate thanks go to God. Thank you God for all those you have placed and will place in my life as I continue this adventure!

INTRODUCTION

This story began to develop on paper for my own therapy back in 1998. Every time I shared a few stories of my life, people would say, "You should write a book."

It was January of 1996 when I started experiencing walking on water. I began to look at my life's challenges as adventures. I felt God was asking me to trust him and walk on water.

This is the story of who I was and of the life lessons that formed me and continue to shape me into the woman God wants me to be.

I have learned we only have today; we can't change the past, and we don't know what will happen in the future. I hope and pray that my story will give you courage in your own life—after all, we are all in this adventure of life together.

CHAPTER 1

GENEALOGY AND CHILDHOOD MEMORIES

I was born in Biloxi on Mississippi's Gulf Coast on November 12, 1956. I am the third of six children: Ricky, Lila, me, Kathy, Mark, and Tina. My mother, Rita Mae Fryou, was one of eight children. My father, Clyde Fredrick Ross, was the youngest boy of fourteen. My grandma Ross had two sets of twins. I had many cousins and most lived nearby.

We lived a simple life. I would now say that we had been poor, but I never thought I needed more than what I had. The house where I grew up was only a few blocks from the Gulf of Mexico. The Gulf Coast was a wonderful place to live as a child. I loved being so close to the water, even with the threat of hurricanes. My father, his father, and four of my father's brothers were shrimpers.

My grandfather had built a forty-two-foot, wood-hull shrimp boat, which my father worked all his life. The boat was the *Mag/Dof*, named after my grandparents, Margaret (Maggie) and Adolph (Doffie). My grandparents owned a little grocery store and had rental property. My grandfather died before I was born.

Grandma Ross was a strong woman; she died in 1983, just short of being ninety-two. She had 55 grandchildren, 108 great-grandchildren, and 19 great-great-grandchildren. I remember when visiting Grandma Ross, we children had to give her a kiss hello and then go outside to play. She had a huge yard with lots of shrubs and trees to get lost in. It was sometimes a little scary for us little kids. Once I slept at her house. When it was close to bedtime, she sat at her beautiful dresser and mirror and took her hair out of its twisted bun and brushed it. She had long beautiful hair, and yet that was the only time I saw it down. She was a quiet, tall woman—a beauty in her day.

One particular summer, Grandma came with us on the boat to Ship Island for the day. She seemed to thoroughly enjoy herself. It was one of those glorious southern summer days, with a light cool breeze and not a cloud in the sky. The water was clear green and the perfect temperature. We anchored near the island, and Dad tied down the ladder. We kids just jumped off the side of the boat and swam around. Dad tied a couple of rafts to a rope and let that drift out for us to hang onto. Grandma wanted to go in the water, but she was not about to jump overboard. Dad and everyone else helped Grandma go slowly down the wobbly ladder. Once she was in the water, holding onto the raft, she was fine. She laughed, and we all had a great time. Getting up the ladder was just as nerve-racking as going down.

My father was fun but very strict. I remember him wrestling with us kids on the floor, tickling us as we squealed with delight.

We would all be jumping on top of each other. The problem was, someone always got hurt, but we loved playing like that. Dad was a big man of six foot two, so I suppose his height intimidated us children. We never gave our mother any trouble when my father was gone, and sometimes he was gone a week or more. We knew that when Dad came home, we would get it. It's funny, Mom never threatened us with "Wait till your dad gets home," and yet, I only remember getting spanked once by him and never by my mom. Waiting in line to be put over his knee was the worst part. We may have only gotten a swat or two, yet his serious face and the matter-of-fact attitude I felt from him meant "I expect you to behave, no ifs, ands, or buts, got it?" It was that good, healthy fear of a parent and a respect for authority that gave me the boundaries that made me feel secure as a young child.

My mom stayed home and cared for us. I never remember coming home to an empty house. Many times I remember smelling beignets or something good cooking as I walked in the door. My mom called her beignets, "poor man's beignets" because she only used self-rising flour and water with a little vanilla—a much cheaper and easier version. My early childhood memories give me great comfort.

My mom was a doer. I have similar traits. I can get caught up in a task—even just cleaning something—and forget everyone else needs to eat or be taken care of. I have gotten better. I can now stop in the middle of a project and walk away.

Mom's dad died when she was a little girl. My Grandma Rita, was a kind, gentle woman. I can remember spending the night at her house. I would get to sleep in her big bed with her, and she would pat my leg till I fell asleep. It was a very comforting place to be, and I felt special there. Grandma had a huge fig tree in her backyard that we used to climb; it was the best. When I was young, we would drop by almost every Sunday after church for a quick visit. She always had something for us to eat. Many times, our cousins would be there too. I have great memories of all of us kids playing in her backyard or running around her wraparound porch and playing hide-and-seek in her front two rooms that were connected to the porch. When we tried running through the house, we were all kicked outside. The porch had a wooden swing, and I remember sitting with my cousins and watching the traffic go by, singing songs and yelling hello to everyone. If we did something wrong when we were there without our parents, grandma would tell us to pick out a switch from a tree, and we would get a swat with it. We learned fast that the larger ones did not hurt as bad as the thinner ones. But it was harder to break the larger twigs.

At one point, Grandma Rita came and lived with us. I remember that she spoke Cajun French to my mom. My mom understood it but did not speak it much. Sometimes I would hear my name in the middle of their conversation, and I would wonder what she was saying about me. The intrigue of knowing a different language, I wish I had learnt when I had the chance. My grandma died fairly young—in her sixties—from emphysema. As a child, it was very difficult to watch her suffer for so long. I wondered why she wouldn't stop smoking.

Over the years I have seen people I love make choices that destroyed their lives in some fashion or other. As I became older, I came to understand how difficult it was to stop an addiction.

I remember our childhood home as modest. We had a small living room, three bedrooms, and one bath. Our kitchen had been small when my parents bought the house, but my father doubled the size of it after a few children. The kitchen was where we really lived—other than outside for us children.

We also had a big front porch. One of the things I liked most about the South was that the weather was nice most of the time. My favorite place was our yard. We had a huge yard. It went from one street to the next street—two-hundred-plus feet. We were rarely given permission to leave the yard, but the neighborhood children could come over. The front yard was open with no trees. We had a chain-link fence all around the property. I loved to do a back bend and crab-walk the length of the yard; I could do cart wheels forever. We would have races, and I was good. What fun memories!

Our front lawn was covered with clover. I would sit on the lawn for hours hunting for a four-leaf clover. On occasion, I would find one. What excitement—a challenge achieved. Amidst the clover were little, white, puff flowers. They had long stems, and we would pick them and tie them to one another to make necklaces, bracelets, and rings—even circles to go around the top of our heads. We felt so pretty. Every time I see a patch of clover, I want to sit in the midst and hunt for a four-leaf clover or make flower chains, but it seems I am always too busy, or perhaps I think I am too old. Maybe one day, I will be able to use the excuse of sitting in the midst of clover with grandchildren.

Summer was always the best. I enjoyed lying on my back and watching the clouds float by. When my sister Kathy was with me, we would yell out the different shapes of animals and other things we saw in the clouds. Oh, those delightful days of summers remembered.

The backyard had lots of shade. We had four large pecan trees. When shrimping season was ending, it was time to collect pecans and crack and hull them. We kids collected them from the yard, and Mom did most of the hulling. We all helped with the cracking of the pecans, but my older sister Lila probably did the most. We used a cool tool: you put one pecan in a slot and pulled down a lever. It was fun at first, but it got old quickly.

Mom made wonderful pies, cake fillings, candies, and cookies once the holidays started coming around. She also would roast pecans in butter and sugar. It was an incredible, mouthwatering treat.

One of my favorite trees had a tire swing. Lots of daydreaming took place in that swing. We all loved being pushed high. We also loved to play house. We girls would rake the leaves into pretend walls for our houses. We always had a kitchen and a bedroom for the babies. We would collect all sorts of things in the yard to pretend to cook. We all remember making our famous mud pies, preparing them just right, decorating them with all sorts of things we collected in the yard, and letting them dry out in the sun. Then the boys would take them and throw them at one another while the girls screamed, "That's our food."

We had a large wood skiff, also in the backyard. When it rained it would fill up. We would stand on the seat and jump in the water that had collected—it was so much fun. I remember leaves would be in the water and little bugs would be swimming around, but it did not matter to us kids. Our backyard was an adventure to be explored.

We had an outside hound dog for quite a few years whose name was Cleo. At one point, we had rabbits and chickens. One day, I observed my Grandma Rita preparing a chicken for our dinner. I saw her wring its neck, and the next time I saw it, it was on my plate for dinner. I did not like that meal—that chicken had been a pet—but still, I didn't say a word. We children always ate what was set before us without a sound. The exception was my younger sister Kathy; she always had a hard time at the dinner table. She did not like vegetables, and she had a strong personality. It's funny, she never out grew it, the not liking vegetables'.

When corn was harvested, we usually got a bushel. We got to help husk the ears, and mom would prepare them for the freezer. My mom and grandma would make tamales and wrap them in the husks of the corn. I loved homemade tamales.

Once, I was in Louisiana visiting family, and we went to a food show; I had the opportunity to eat alligator. It tasted like chicken and so did frog legs. I remember having turtle soup. My father had caught a huge turtle in the ocean. It was actually good.

My parents were adamant about never wasting things. My brother Ricky was allowed to shoot his BB gun in the backyard and kill birds and squirrels, but the rule was, whatever you killed, you had to eat. I remember watching him clean those critters and prepare a little fire outside to cook them. He acted like the meal was great, but I never tried it.

I vividly remember peeling potatoes with a knife (we did not own a peeler), and my father would stand over us saying that we were wasting too much of the potato. You just did not waste things in my family. I did eventually master peeling a potato the way my father liked. I own a peeler now, which is a great tool I might add.

Seafood was often on the table. A few times, my father brought home a cowfish, which was interesting looking. Its head was shaped like a cow's head with little horns. The body was a hard shell—only the fins and tail were soft. You had to use a hammer to break the hard shell, and when you pulled on the tail, a large lump of meat was attached. It tasted very good. We ate shark too, but only a certain kind. Another favorite was the eggs, called roe, of a mullet, a fish caught with a net cast into the Gulf. During certain times of the year, you could even catch shrimp if the net had smaller holes. We had fried squid, but that was not my favorite. When my father came home from a shrimping trip, he would bring ice chests full of shrimp and crabs and fish to be taken care of. Everything had to be cleaned and packaged to be put in the freezer for the winter and spring.

Cleaning the seafood was a necessary part of any seafood meal, and we all helped. Squid were fun to clean. You first pull off the head. That is where the ink is. There is a feather in the body that you have to pull out. Pull the outer skin off and then slice it into rings. It was funny, I had a hard time with the chicken, but cleaning seafood was never a problem. Preparing a soft-shell crab was another interesting job. Once, the crab was still alive, and when I started to cut it, it moved, and I jumped. I had to put it in the fridge for a little while longer. I couldn't cut its head off while it was still alive. Picking boiled crabs, which was removing the meat, was a workout until you got the knack of it. It took time and patience.

No matter what the task, everyone always helped. I'm sure Mom did so much more since she had to keep us busy. Especially now that I am a mother, I see the amount of work it takes to keep everyone on task. Mom probably could have done things faster without our help. I see the value in taking the time to train the kids—it trained me to be more patient, which I have not totally perfected yet. I believe those were the life skills—hard work and perseverance—that really formed me into the person I am today.

Lila, Kathy, and I shared a room. At one point, three of us slept in a double bed. When Tina was about two, she came to stay with us in our room. Lila had her own twin bed, and Tina slept with her. Kathy and I came up with a plan for the double bed we shared; we had an invisible line we could not cross over. What silly girls we were. I suppose we just knew we needed space, and as long as we respected each other's space, we had a good relationship.

Our room was always neat. We were taught to make our beds at an early age. I later learned that my mom would often remake our beds and straighten up. When we came home from school, our room was always in order. Even in the summer, she must have straightened up after we went outside to play, because I always remember our room being neat.

We owned two or three dresses each, which our mom made for us, and the dresses usually matched. We went to Mass every Sunday and were always dressed up. We may have looked like ragamuffins during the week, but Sunday was special. To this day, that's how I feel about Sunday and church. We all had one pair each of dress shoes, sneakers, and possibly flip flops for the summer. I remember having rubber jelly shoes on a few summers, which were lots of fun. When we were home we did not have to wear shoes outside. I liked not wearing shoes. With all the clover outside, bees were always around in the summer. I was teased about how I walked on my tiptoes all the time. I believed that if you walked on your toes, you wouldn't get stung, but I still did. When it happened, Mom would sit me on the counter and break open one of her cigarettes, wet it, and put it on my sting. I was told the tobacco drew the poison out, and it did always feel better.

I liked our room. We girls had the largest of the three bedrooms. One summer, mom had sewed matching curtains and bedspreads for our two trundle beds. We each had our own bed finally, yoo-hoo. The fabric was lightweight, off-white cotton, and she ironed stencils on it. She used painting tubes and painted the patterns. I was so proud of our room. The design was the mod dolls that were popular in the late '60s. Lila and I drew and colored different-sized flowers on paper and cut them out and tacked them all over the walls. I still vividly remember the room. It was a great summer project that year.

In the summer, we did chores every day in the morning before we could play outside. Saturday was the big day for heavy cleaning. We had to clean everything thoroughly, and the kitchen had to be mopped. We waxed the floors by hand on our knees. You could eat off the floors, and they looked incredibly shiny.

Lila was a great example to me. My father called her Cinderella because she was always working. On ironing day, we would spray starch on the clothes, roll them up tight, and put them in the refrigerator veggie drawers. We didn't have a dryer and the cloths were always stiff and wrinkly; then along came polyester—hooray.

I loved our front porch; even when it rained, we could be outside. We played many board games there. One year we played gin rummy all summer long. I think it taught me to count faster and to think faster so I could process what strategy I would use.

Playing games taught me to be a good sport, which is a valuable lesson for life. One summer, about six of us kids in the neighborhood got together every Sunday and had a never-ending monopoly game. We would play for a couple of hours at a time. Our friends' parents let us keep the game up; it was great. I learned how to be honest and how to win or lose graciously. The kids I hung around with and my siblings never thought about cheating—it was wrong, period. I had good role models as a child. We mostly just had fun and laughed a lot.

My mom always cooked big, hot meals for both lunch and dinner every day. Sandwiches were not in our meal plans much. If we were having sandwiches, she would grind up chicken or ham, making it into a spread.

Mom would call us in for lunch, and we would eat as a family. We prayed and thanked God at every meal. After eating, we would clean the kitchen and go back out to play. If we got thirsty while we were playing, we would just drink from the hose. It was great.

Many times, Mom would bring shampoo and soap outside, and we would have our baths under the hose. One summer, we had a Slip 'n Slide, which we played with for hours at a time. Sprinklers were always fun, running crazily with my siblings in and out of the spraying water screeching with delight. Another summer, we got a pool—one that went up to my chest. We would make a circle train going around the pool until it made a current strong enough so we could just float and let it carry us. There was lots of laughter, and we had a great deal of fun with it for a few years.

CHAPTER 2

SUMMERS ON THE WATER

My father did not like the highways. He was most comfortable when he was driving the boat; he knew the waters.

Once, we went to Louisiana to visit relatives. My father made a wrong turn on the highway, and it was not easy to turn back around. We heard his frustration for quite a while! I almost wanted to walk the rest of the way. Needless to say, we did not go away to visit very often.

For many summers, we went out on the boat for a week or more as our family vacation. There was an island, which took us about an hour to get to, called Ship Island. The east part of the island was called Quarantine. During the war, they had built houses and a hospital for the transitioning of the sick. It had a man-made cove, which offered a little protection from the Gulf and a pier to tie up to. There was an artesian well on the island.

That was the best water ever for drinking. When we would take our showers in the evenings it was a little cold, but we endured it and made it fun. No other boats normally stayed overnight, so we had the island to ourselves most of the time.

On a few occasions, other relatives would come out with their families, which meant more cousins to play with, building sand castles and chasing each other in the water. We were able to go swimming anytime we wanted, and we did lots of exploring on the island.

On occasion, our family would go on walks, and my father would name everything and tell us about everything he saw.

My mom always made good food. On the way out to the island, my father would drop a "try troll," a smaller net that my dad used to check if there were any shrimp in the area. We would catch just enough seafood for us. My mom would cook anything edible. Fresh seafood was the best. Mom brought the hand-crank ice cream maker, and for a treat we would make a few batches of the most delicious ice cream you ever tasted. We usually made one plain vanilla and then one with fruit in it. We would take turns cranking or sitting on the ice cream maker. The sitting job was cold sometimes, but there was a towel over it, and that helped. There was always great excitement over the creamy goodness that was to come.

The boat had a huge ice hold, which was where we kept the food that needed to stay cold. We also had a chest-type ice box on the back of the boat with doors that slid open for smaller items. This was for daily foods like milk, eggs, bacon, and cheese.

There were always a couple of watermelons for the trip in the ice hold. When we ate watermelon we would put our whole face right into the slice and have juice all over our faces and dripping down our arms. Then we had the joy of jumping off the boat to clean off. There was a hose on the boat that pulled up the ocean water, and my dad used it to clean the boat off after his shrimping trips. Sometimes he would turn that hose on us and wash us down. It had a strong flow, and there was a lot of squealing from us kids.

My older brother Ricky had a skiff with a small motor, and we got to go for rides in it on occasion. When Mark, my youngest brother was old enough, he would take us for rides too. Fishing off the back of Dad's boat was always exciting. Ricky and Mark enjoyed fishing more than the girls did, because when we caught something, we didn't want to take it off the hook. Those fish wiggled too much. I did eventually grow out of that. Throwing our fishing lines sometimes became dangerous too.

The pilothouse had three bunks, and there were extra mattresses. The floor shape of the house was a capital I, and my dad would put the mattresses in a T shape for us girls. The space he left open was where the bathroom was. My two brothers got to sleep in a tent—once they set it up on the front of the boat, and another time they set it up on the pier. I think they liked being on the pier the best. There seemed to be a nice breeze off the water once the sun went down. We had little fans, so at least air was moving. It was pretty comfortable for us kids, but I'm not sure how it was for my parents. A storm came through one time, yet I felt safe. We kids stayed in our beds. My father stayed up checking the ropes and securing things so they wouldn't fly away. Storms usually did not last long.

In June, there was always the Blessing of the Fleet. The tradition had started when all of the boats would get blessed for the new shrimping season. A train of boats would drive by a big boat that was anchored with a priest on it. He would sprinkle holy water out to the boat and give a blessing, and we would all kneel solemnly and bless ourselves. Then we would anchor close to Deer Island, a barrier island, and go to the shore and play the rest of the afternoon.

We usually had other families with us on day trips. We would leave early in the morning and go to the west end of Ship Island where there was a fort. That was where most of the boaters went. My mom would make a huge pot of chili, and each family would bring their own hot dogs and buns. The minute we left the dock, we were making chili dogs and getting a Barq's root beer. That could have been as early as eight in the morning.

Barq's originated in Biloxi, Mississippi, and we used to go to the plant and get cases of it, which lasted a long time. As kids, we were not allowed to just take a soda whenever we wanted one; even on the boat, we knew there was a limit.

Once we got our food, we would go to the back of the boat and sit with our legs dangling off. The water would splash up at times and we would get all wet. Occasionally, we would get old bread and throw it to the seagulls. Watching them catch the bread in midair was so much fun. We would often catch a glimpse of dolphins running alongside the boat. Before we were old enough to go to the back of the boat, our spot had been on the front bow. That was fun too. Sometimes the water would splash up in our faces with lots of squealing. The water at Ship Island was a beautiful green and clear. Biloxi's water was more of a brown color, maybe because of all the turmoil of the boats and the shrimp factories along the water's edge. Deer Island also kept the water from not getting cleaned out as much. But it was important for Biloxi as it helped keep the city safer from storms.

When the Fourth of July came, we did a similar thing: got up early and headed out to Ship Island with a boat full of people and lots of good food. On those days, we got to stay a lot longer because the fireworks off Deer Island weren't until dark. The other families would bring all sorts of good food to share anytime they came with us on the boat. We would have fried chicken, barbecued ribs or chicken, and baked chicken, which the moms had cooked that morning—what a work of love. Potato salads, coleslaw, chips and cookies, a few pies, and cakes, with one usually decorated for the Fourth of July, were always on hand. We had banana pudding (the real homemade kind) and, of course, some watermelons. And there was the huge pot of the best chili, which my mom cooked. Those were great days.

When we settled in for the fireworks, the older kids got to go on top of the pilothouse, and we would lay there and watch. You felt you could almost touch them. For me, it was like touching heaven. *Ooh's* and *aah's* followed the spectacular colors of the fireworks; they were so close, and it was incredible. On occasion, a spark would land on the boat and would need to be put out. We never saw any real danger though. I have never experienced fireworks the same way: being on a boat with the colors exploding right above me. My memories of those summers as a child still make me smile.

Once, when I was a little older, maybe ten, I got to take a shrimping trip with my dad and my brother Ricky. I learned what hard work was all about. Dad put the nets overboard, and we waited thirty to forty minutes. When he picked up the net, he would dump it on the deck, and we would have to sit on a small stool in the midst of all those creatures and separate the good fish, the shrimp, and the crab from what they called "the trash." Crabs were crawling everywhere, and the fish were flopping all over the place. Sometimes, a pretty big shark, a stingray or even an eel would be in the net. Dad took care of the big things. The sea gulls would go crazy, flying around and waiting for us to throw the fish we didn't want over the side. We would have a scooper in one hand, which was a flat blade on a handle; we used it to pull small amounts of the seafood toward us and pick the good stuff out. We didn't use gloves, I might add. While we were separating the seafood, the nets would go back overboard. By the time we finished cleaning up, it was time for another net to be dumped. This lasted all night because the shrimp were more plentiful at night.

When we arrived at the dock after the long night of work, we had to haul the ice chest to the truck. The pier was being worked on at that time, and in one section it was only a board you walked across. I was helping my father carry the ice chest, which probably weighed more than me, and I lost my balance and fell into the water. It was the grossest water ever—diesel fuel, dead fish, and murky mud that I sank in almost to my knees. Just thinking about it makes me shiver. The ice chest was saved, and there was no lost seafood. I wasn't hurt, so no time to make a scene; we had work to do. To this day, I still struggle with that "Let's get the job done no matter what". It isn't a bad thing; it just needs balance.

CHAPTER 3

SCHOOL DAYS

I attended a public school, which was a block away from our house. The name of my school was Dukate Elementary. There was an empty lot in front of our house. I could see our school from our front door. School was not my favorite to begin with, probably due to the fact I experienced children who were not very kind.

My parents had not finished school; they had had to work at an early age. They did not help us with any homework whatsoever. There was never any push to do well. Whatever we did was good enough. At home was where I learned "Just do your best at whatever you do." My parents focused on our chores and responsibilities and respect for our elders. I believe I learned more at home than school. I did not read leisurely, and I don't remember any books in our home. My children, on the other hand, had many books.

One of my memories of school was during recess, a few of

us girls would pile up leaves and make pretend walls and play house, cooking all sorts of things. Playing on the swings or other playground things were taken by the faster and more aggressive children. I experienced a lot of teasing from the other kids, which started around fifth or sixth grade. I had grown to five foot six and weighed all of about eighty-five pounds. I was all arms and legs—a sight to behold. In sixth grade, I was part of the track team. I had these long legs, and I was pretty fast. On the day of the meet, I woke up sick and could not go. I can still see myself standing at the door, looking at all the people going to the school for the track meet. I was very sad and disappointed.

Our elementary school had the most incredible Christmas pageant. It was the highlight of my years in elementary school. The whole school would depict the Nativity. To the side of the stage was a large, wooden, half-circle, six-tier, live-angel tree stand. You had to be in fifth or sixth grade to be toward the top. We angels were dressed in white gowns and wearing halos. We sang about four songs. The angel standing on the top sang a solo part and got to have wings. The top three tiers had a little holding rail. I once got to be on the tier three down from the top, which was pretty high up. It was an awesome experience. We also held candles, real candles. At one point a candle was lit at the bottom, and a trail of lights went up the tree to the top angel. Kids may have been more responsible in the sixties, but I have to add some were still unkind.

Getting ready for Christmas was an incredibly exciting time. It is sad how much has been lost over the years. Honoring God our maker should be important in a public school. He sent his Son to save us. Where have we gone wrong?

As a child, I sat on the couch and stared at the Christmas tree lights, getting lost in my own little world. It was so magical and exciting. The smells associated with preparing for Christmas included all the baking my mom did. She had big, two-gallon jars, and she would fill them with all sorts of cookies and treats and put them in the freezer until Christmas. Just before Christmas, she would put tablecloths on the washer and dryer (which were in the kitchen) and on the big chest freezer. All of the cakes, pies, and cookies would be set out from Christmas Eve to New Year's Day. We children ate many times a day from those goodies.

To this day, I associate yummy smells to those fun days of my youth. That memory made me want to have yummy smells for my own children when they came home from school. My favorites were "poor man's" beignets, chocolate chip cookies, and banana bread. Once, my son Josh ran in the house yelling, "I could smell the beignets all the way down the street." I enjoyed bringing smiles to their faces.

CHAPTER 4

HURRICANE CAMILLE

When I was twelve, my family's life was drastically changed by Hurricane Camille, and it affected our family for years to come. It was the summer before I went to my new school, Central Junior High, where I would be in seventh grade.

Hurricane Camille hit Mississippi's Gulf Coast on August 17, 1969. It was early evening, right before dark, and my father was watching the news on the TV. He and my mother were discussing the approaching storm. My mom was pleading with my father saying, "Some of the neighbors are going across the street." There was a two-story, cinder-block mission church across the street. She ended with, "Clyde, we can't keep the children here."

We lived only a few blocks from the Gulf. My father reluctantly agreed to go across the street. We children were told to put a few things together, only the necessities. I had a special Winnie the

Pooh bear I didn't want to get ruined. I decided that the top shelf in the bathroom was the highest place in the house to keep him. As we were walking across the street, it was raining a little, and I heard my father say to my mom, "That's salt water flowing on the ground." He took my older brother Ricky, who was sixteen, back to the house with him to put things higher up. My father grew up on the water; it was his whole life. I remember wondering how he knew that it was salt water, but something inside me knew he knew.

We children were having a great time playing games with the neighborhood kids. Then we heard the grown-ups talking about putting the children and women in the attic if the water got to the last step. It was three steps away. All of a sudden, I realized my mom was crying. My dad and Ricky had not come back from the house. The whole mood of the evening changed for everyone. Some of the men took lanterns out on the balcony that faced our house, trying to see something. At that time, the eye of the storm was passing, and it was calm outside and not raining. The men on the balcony saw someone approach from the water. It was my father and brother.

Our home had turned sideways and had been swept two lots over. They saw the lights behind them and swam towards the light. My father said the water had surged in so fast that they could not leave. They had clung to the half-screened porch of our home until the eye of the storm was passing, because it was calmer. At one point, my brother had gone under, and my father had grasped an electrical wire for support and grabbed my brother. Trash was floating by them, and the current was strong. Because the house had moved, they did not know where they were going until they reached the neighbors on the porch. It was an incredible reunion for the family. The water never got to the last step.

Early the next morning, everyone went out to assess the damage. I was old enough to go. My parents had just bought a new station wagon a couple of days earlier. Our yard in the back of the house was on an incline. My parents had parked the new car, my brother's car, and my dad's truck back there. The truck was the only vehicle that was okay. The water had not gotten to its engine like it did to the smaller cars.

We saw a house on top of two cars in the middle of the street. One house, two lots over, was not there anymore. We heard of a neighbor who tried to hang onto a tree and died. It was incredible; debris was everywhere, in some places four or five feet high. We had to climb over all sorts of things. Cars were piled on top of each other.

Inside our house there was mud, sea grass, and trash piled two or more feet deep in places. The freezer and refrigerator had turned over. As I walked by my room, I saw all my stuffed animals on the bed; nothing had happened to them. The mattresses had floated. I ran to the back of the house where the bathroom was and realized that the water line was higher in the back of the house as compared to the front. My bear was ruined. I was crushed.

That was one of the first lessons of life that left a mark on my heart. As an adult, I realized I needed to be detached, to not try to hold onto things or allow things to control me when the loss of those things would take away my joy that was from God. This didn't mean I shouldn't grieve or feel sad about something. We all have feelings; God made us that way. But if something draws us away from God, and our goal is to go to heaven, we would have allowed something to interfere with our goal, not trusting in his bigger plan for our life.

That lesson prepared me for bigger things. I needed to be aware of not allowing anything to become more important than

God was in my life. God needed to be first in all areas of my life. When God was first, all my other relationships were better.

My father went to check on his boat as soon as the roads were somewhat cleared. The boat fared well. It became our transportation. We had an aunt and uncle who did not have any damage; they lived on the other side of the bay in Ocean Springs. Bridges were out, but we could get there by boat, and so we ended up staying with our relatives across the bay for a short time. Then we moved into a nearby house for a couple of months. The state put together a trailer complex in a park close to our home. We were able to move there, which made it easier for my parents to work on our house. It was a three-bedroom trailer. Our family of eight people made it pretty tight. I don't remember being there very much. It was a safe place to sleep and was very close to our house and our school. School did not start right away; it took a few months. My father, brother, and relatives gutted our home and, amazingly, put it back together rather quickly. We had relatives who did electrical work and others who did plumbing. Looking back, God had provided us many people with diverse talents. Instead of sheetrock, which took a lot of work and time, my father used paneling, which was easier and faster. Our home had to be moved back onto our property. In the process of the move, they dropped the house, and it broke a few windows. No windows had been broken during the storm, and my father wasn't too happy. During all those months of fixing the house, my father could not work much on the boat, which meant no income.

Once the house was put back together, we all moved back home. Little by little, the added toil and the degree to which the storm affected my father began to show. My parents had just finished paying off the mortgage. This set them back financially, as they had to start all over again and get another mortgage. I believe that the trauma my father went through on the front porch that night during the storm deeply affected him.

My father had always provided financially for my grandmother. Anytime he worked on the boat it was split three ways: one for the boat, one for him, and one for his mother. As a child, I saw him change. I know now that he had lost hope, and despair set in. He had no joy of the Lord. He allowed worries and concerns to consume him. He did not trust in God. My parents' relationship slowly deteriorated. They drew away from their faith and the sacraments. Things gradually changed. My father began to drink more and more, spending his time staring at the TV.

This is probably one of the reasons I have a problem with TVs and with alcohol. I saw them control my father. I never wanted anything to control me like that. My mother had been a chain smoker since she was fourteen, and I saw how that controlled her, which was very sad for me.

My parents' fighting had been a rare thing when I was younger. Life had changed, as a young teenager, I did not understand the pain my parents were going through.

CHAPTER 5

JUNIOR HIGH

Junior high was a hard time for me. It was the first year that the school system integrated the schools, mixing black and white children. At that time of my life, my father was prejudiced. I was not sure what to expect, because I had experienced that the white children in elementary school were not very kind. I was worried the junior high children might be worse. I met some very nice black girls and realized it wasn't the color of your skin that defined who you were. It was your attitude and how you treated other people. My world opened up that year. I did meet a friend in junior high, Ann, who was an only child. We are still close forty-plus years later.

There was one incident in seventh grade that I remember vividly. I was in the lunch room. There was a box for anyone to submit information for the school newsletter. Girls started writing so-and-so loves so-and-so. One of the tougher white girls in my class got the idea that I wrote that she loved this very large black guy, and she was mad and kept badgering me. She wouldn't believe me that I did not do that. It got so bad that I felt I was up against a wall, and I blurted out, "Okay, okay. I'll meet you behind the little grocery store after school." This was where all the fights took place.

I could not believe I had said that. I had never done anything like that before. My stomach was in knots, but by the time school was over, I was mad that had she put me in a situation I did not want to be in. When we met behind the store, I beat her up, mostly by slapping her, and because I had long fingernails, she got all scratched up. She finally yelled for me to stop, and I did. I remember just running home, all six blocks. By the time I got home, my heart was racing crazily. When I walked in the house, my younger siblings were watching a cartoon. I sat in my little brother's wooden rocker, rocking and trying to calm down, hoping no one would notice my breathing. I never told anyone in my family. I did not want to remember that event. I was ashamed of my behavior.

The next day at school, the girl I had the fight with approached me and wanted to be my friend. I thought, *To be your friend I needed to beat you up?* That's not how I wanted to make friends.

It was also in junior high school that I got into the habit of cursing. I suppose it is a stage everyone goes through, but the way my two girlfriends and I chose to break this habit was unusual. We walked to school every day. We decided to punch each other in the arm when we slipped. I was probably all of eighty-five pounds then, and it hurt when those girls punched me. I was cured of that habit quickly. As I look back, I think I was already somewhat formed in my thinking. I was determined, and I knew instinctively how crude and unladylike it was. It was a hard age—when we were coming into ourselves and making choices, everything seemed so confusing. I am grateful to God that my two friends were such good influences at the time.

CHAPTER 6

HIGH SCHOOL

The summer before my senior year, I worked at a shrimp factory. I learned a huge life lesson that summer. My mother would get me up at three in the morning to go to the factory. It smelled, and it was hot. I would stand with a large metal trash can next to me, and I would "headless " the shrimp. I got to be pretty fast, and I learned how to use both hands at the same time. The heads would go in the trash can, and we would get paid for how many pounds of heads we picked. Other times, I would stand next to a belt and sift through the seafood that passed by on the belt, taking out the fish and any trash. We worked eight to ten hours on most days. I found out later mom did not need to work. She just did it so I could work to make money for a car.

One of the most memorable times with my parents was when they took me to the car dealership. We found an awesome black mustang with a white hardtop, 1968 and very plush. It even had electric windows. I was flying—that car was so cool. I remember arguing with my father right before summer, saying that I needed a car. He stuck to his guns and told me to get a job first. I did not understand his thinking, but he was right. God took care of everything. The school helped me get a job at a nearby grocery store right before school started. It was a work program for students not planning on going to college. I was happy to not have to be at school all day. The school was big, and the few friends I had I never saw at school.

As I became older, I started remembering specific incidents that demonstrated my mom's true nature; she was a quiet woman of selflessness, even with food. She always bought a whole chicken and cut it up, as she said it was cheaper. She ate the backbone of the chicken and a wing. After we all grew up and left home, she would order the breast when we got fried chicken for a family get-together. I remember asking, "You don't like white meat, do you?" She shared with us that she only ate the boney pieces because that was all that was left after we all had our plates. In our house, mom served everyone's plate, and then she served herself last. I would be happy to have half the mindset of that selfless giving I now recognize in my mom.

Ricky and his wife Debbie had a little girl, Dawn, she was about four months old. When I was a senior I often went to their house to sleep and take care of Dawn the next day. In the morning, I would get the car started and turn the heater on when it was a little chilly. One day, I got Dawn situated in her car seat, buckled her in, locked the electric door locks on the passenger side, and closed the door. She was safe and sound. Wrong. The keys were in the ignition, and the car was running, securely locked with Dawn inside. I freak out for a second and then ran in the house to call my mom who was only two minutes from us. When I got back outside, Dawn was screaming, and her little knit cap had slipped down over her eyes. It was a sight to behold. I felt so helpless. But I knew my mom was coming soon, and she arrived with the extra keys three minutes later. It was the longest five minutes of my life, and it took a long time to get over that experience.

CHAPTER 7

MEETING THE RIGHT GUY

In October of my senior year, I met my husband-to-be, David Arguelles. He was in his first year of junior college in our town. We had gone to the same high school, but he had been a year ahead of me. The school was very large. He had grown up four blocks from me, but I never knew him. He went to an elementary Catholic school, and we had gone to different Catholic churches.

My friend Ann and I had gone to our school football game. At the end of the game, we became separated while walking down the bleachers. I ended up next to a cute boy who talked to me. When I found my friend, I asked her if she knew who that boy was. Her comment was, "Oh yeah, that's Michael's little brother." Michael was three years older than us. I couldn't get that cute boy out of my mind. When homecoming rolled around, I decided to call him. It was proper to invite a boy to something at your school if he did not go to your school. I sat on the floor of my brother Mark's room with the door closed. Our phone had a six-foot-long extension cord. Butterflies were taking over my stomach as I dialed his number. I told him who I was and asked if he knew me.

He responded, "Yes, I do."

I was jumping in my skin, *He knows me; he knows me.*

When I asked him if he would be my date for prom, he responded quickly, "Sure."

But that's not the end of the story. My dear friend Ann was dating someone, and they decided to have his friend take me, and we would all double-date. When I told her about my date with David, she said, "Oh no, you are going with [so and so]."

We had a long telephone conversation arguing about it, but she won. Her date, who was also a friend of David, would explain the problem to him. Then, as happens with all teenagers who have complicated lives, my date and his girlfriend got back together. Ann decided that her date should ask David if he would still go out with me.

Fortunately, David said yes again. I should have known then what a wonderful and easygoing person he was. He was going to need it with me.

On our first date, when David took me to the door to say goodnight, all he did was say goodnight and ask if he could call me. I remember running to my room and jumping on my bed, so excited that he did not try to kiss me. I had only been out with a couple of guys, and one in particular was a memory I would have rather not remembered. He had roaming hands, and I was exhausted from trying to keep his hands off me. I was glad we had been double-dating, as that helped some. I went out with him only once.

After knowing David for only two months, I knew I wanted to spend the rest of my life with him. During the two years we dated, I came alive. I had never experienced being so loved.

My parents had started fighting more, and I was ready to get out. At the time, I had not realized the toil that the hurricane had taken on my parents and their relationship. Living at home had become hard with all the arguing. Being a teenager in that turmoil was difficult.

For Christmas, David gave me a promise ring. It had two little stones, and I was so excited. My mom made the comment, "Where is it?" teasing me because it was so small. To me, it was the love and commitment behind the ring, not what it looked like.

I am ashamed to say that David and I did not stay pure. I wish I had known my dignity and the sacredness of a conjugal relationship within the sacrament of marriage as a teenager, but I didn't. We were not aware of the pitfalls of placing yourself in temptation's way. But what is interesting is that something happened, and we realized it was wrong; in the six months before we were married, we decided to stay pure. It was not easy, because we had gotten too comfortable with one another, and we were very young. And the turmoil at home was pushing me more into his arms. We needed to stay on guard and avoid situations where we might be tempted, like being alone. I thank God for that time of self-sacrifice in preparing for the holy sacrament of marriage. I really experienced true love from David in those six months.

As a child, my parents took us to church and made sure we received all the sacraments. But I really did not know much about my faith. As an adult and having had so much happen to me, I know now that you need more; for the sacraments to come alive, you need to live them. I knew and believed that there was a God, Jesus, and the Holy Spirit. I realize now that you also need a real relationship with God the Father, Jesus, and the Holy Spirit. That's what my father and mother had needed when life came at them. And life does come.

Chapter 8

Marriage and Growing Up

I graduated from high school in 1974. I married my best friend in October of 1975. I was eighteen, almost nineteen, and Dav had just turned twenty. We lived in a little row house, right next to the railroad tracks, for three months. In a row house, you have to walk through one room to get to the next. In ours, there was the living room, the bedroom, the bathroom, and then the kitchen. So if we had guests, they would have to go through our bedroom to get to either the kitchen or the living room. When the train went by, if we had dishes setting out to drain, more than likely they would be on the floor. It was a fun time—our own little space. Most of our furnishings had been given to us, and we had bought an old iron bed from some aunts for almost nothing. We were happy.

Then we moved to Mobile, Alabama, for Dav to finish school at South Alabama. It was a long, hard, three years. In the beginning, Dav did great; he made the dean's list. We had decided I would work, and he would focus on school. The burden of the finances on just me was incredible. We were so poor that we ate French-fry sandwiches many times. A ten-pound bag of potatoes was only a dollar or two, and we reused the grease over and over. At times, the family would ask us to visit and they would offer to pay for the gas. Both of our parents would send us home with bags of food. At one point, we got food stamps, but that was hard, because one of us needed to spend time going to the Social Security office, which neither of us had the time to do. The first year was a killer; we were either going to make it or it would break us, which it almost did. I became very depressed. I had married this great guy, but he was never around. He was studying all the time. I was very young. When we had dated during those first two years he was in college, I saw him all the time. But this university was very hard, and he wanted to do well. I wanted him to do well too, but I was immature. I started seeking fun with the people at work, which was not a good thing.

One night, it all came to a head. I had been out, and it was very late and I had gotten lost. I was alone and scared. I really didn't know anyone well. I ended up calling Dav, crying that I was lost. He asked me to tell him the things around me, and he figured out where I was. He came and got me, and I followed him home. I wanted to leave and go back to Biloxi. This was not the life I wanted. We stayed up all night talking, and the bottom line for him was, "I don't believe in divorce; what can I do?" I suppose I didn't either, but everything was way too hard.

I finally said, "You have to spend time with me, and you need to get a part-time job." He did not make the dean's list anymore, but he still did well. He got a part-time job, which made it longer to finish school.

We became very creative, doing things that did not cost much money. We would have a candlelight dinner in the living room on the floor at the coffee table; it was very quaint, with a simple meal. We would go to the beach for the day with an ice chest of food and a six pack of beer (a rare treat). We learned how to dig two holes next to each other and lay a sheet over them for our chairs.

God opened a door for me to change jobs—the opportunity literally fell in my lap. It was at a great bank in the accounting department. The manager was the kindest father figure I have ever experienced in the work field. The people were family-oriented, and they were a good example for me.

It took six months or more for our relationship to resume as husband and wife. I think of it as the "rekindling the coals" time. Because that's what our relationship had become, lukewarm coals that needed lots of work to get going again. I can honestly say that I did not love Dav anymore. I was confused and really hurting. I knew in my heart that I couldn't give up; it was not in me to give up. But it was Dav's determination that pushed me on. He was very patient with me and loved me unconditionally. I know now that that was the first time I experienced God's love. Dav and I grew up together and learned a lot about survival in relationships. Little did I realize, God was preparing us for more.

I remember a time when God taught me something, but I didn't realize he was teaching me at the time. Early in our marriage, we were sitting at my parents' kitchen table, and behind me was the sink. I asked Dav to get me a glass of water. He was across the table from me, on the other side, and the sink was right behind me. I had a thought later. *Why did I do that?* I realized I had wanted my father to see that I was not going to let Dav boss me around.

I had observed my parents in their relationship and saw how my mother walked around on eggshells, making sure my father was happy. She fixed all his meals and his coffee, and my father even told my mom when it was time to go to bed. She was caring for someone to keep peace, which did not work anyway, versus doing it out of love. Then I realized that Dav and I didn't have that kind of relationship. I would not want him to treat me like that, so why should I treat him like that?

Once, when we were going to Biloxi for Easter, I had set the bag of gifts for our families by the back door for Dav to put in the car. We got to Biloxi, and I asked, "Where is the bag with the gifts?"

Dav asked, "What bag?"

I replied, "The one by the back door."

He had thought it was garbage, and he had thrown it out. That was an interesting Easter—no gifts for the parents, nieces, and nephews. Thank God, we eventually laughed about the whole thing. When Dav was younger, his job at home had been to put the garbage out; he had had a habit of not doing it. One morning, his mom put the bags in the bed with him to remind him. So I suppose he had learned to be efficient. Well, that time he was too efficient.

Not long after I started my job with the bank, I started having trouble with my health. My esophagus would close up, and I could not breathe; my heart would pound rapidly, my fingers would get numb, and I would feel tingling all over my body. It would take hours or even a full day to recuperate from the trauma on my body. I went through some extensive tests and was told I was allergic to cigarette smoke. The girl who sat next to me smoked at her desk after lunch. I had grown up with smoking—my mom was a chain smoker—so it was the last thing on my mind. The doctor said my body had gotten used to not being around the smoke those couple of years and was rebelling, not wanting it in my body again. I found out later that some cigarettes are worse than others. If I didn't have a full-blown attack, I would pay dearly with horrendous headaches, which sometimes lasted for days. This changed our lives drastically.

We got through the college years. By the time Dav graduated, we were in a good place together. We still had things to learn; we had stopped going to Mass, mostly because we did not find a church we felt comfortable in. Now I realize that that is really not a good reason. Going to church is not about how it makes you feel; it's an overflow of the personal relationship you have with God. We did not have a relationship with God, which was really the key. When we went home to Biloxi, we always went with his family on Sunday. God was always there but not invited into our life.

After graduation, Dav was offered jobs in California, Texas, Alabama, and Florida—we chose Florida. Pensacola Beach was only two hours from Biloxi. We loved the water and the white sand beaches. I got a job at a bank and was happy.

CHAPTER 9

TRAGEDY

Tragedy happened shortly after our move to Florida. The three years we were away at college were very rocky for my parents. We received a call that my younger brother Mark, who was sixteen, had shot himself and was in the hospital in critical condition.

My mother had left home and had gone to her sister's house to get away from the fighting. She had brought Tina, who was fourteen, with her. When Mark walked in the house from being out that night, my father was home. All we knew was that my father heard a gunshot; he was the one who called 911. They had to bring my father to a mental hospital because he was so out of control. At one point, we believed my father had shot our brother, but we realized later that was not the case. My brother had had his own issues, on top of the issues with our parents' problems. Mark lived for five days; he lost one lung, and there was a pinhole in other one, but the doctors did not know it. When they took him off the respirator, his other lung collapsed, and he died.

At Mark's funeral, I became emotionally distraught, crying so much that I began to hyperventilate. They took me out of the main room, trying to console me about Mark. I blurted out, "No, No, No, I want my daddy back the way he was." I just kept repeating it.

I noticed some of the relatives moved away. I felt I was too much for them. I ended up going to counseling after that for about six months, and they put me on something to help me stay focused, but I did not like anything controlling me. I was off the medication within six months, which was not easy, because once you are on medication, it's hard to wean off. Life keeps going.

That was the beginning of the outward destruction of my family.

My parents divorced—the first of three times from each other in a timeframe of ten to twelve years. I remember that first divorce. I was twenty-one and had been married for a few years. I had a life, but my emotional response was that my father had abandoned me. This was not good. I was very confused and deeply hurting.

The last time they divorced, I heard from my siblings that my father had given us children an ultimatum: choose me or your mother. That was not something any of us could do, so none of us had a relationship with our father after that time.

CHAPTER 10

GROWING AS A FAMILY

Dav and I had rented an apartment for a short time. Then it was time to be homeowners. We bought a house and added a screened-in porch. To open up the living room, we knocked out a wall and had a stone fireplace put in the corner. We did some updating to the kitchen. That's when we realized that we liked building together. We made a good team. I learned how to lay bricks and put up sheetrock. We had fun and learned a lot together. Two years later, we were buying property on a cul-de-sac and getting a house built. We did all of the painting of the cabinets, walls, and trim in order to lower the cost of the house. We wanted to be involved in this dream home. We were busy and loving the challenge.

We did not have much faith at that time; we were floating around and still not drawn to go to church. We decided to adopt.

We started the process with Catholic Social Services. One of the criteria's for adoption was to have a priest know you. That meant we needed to be going to church regularly. We found a church near our home, Nativity of Our Lord, and we started attending. Dav got involved with the Holy Name Society, a group of men he clicked with. I started teaching a kindergarten CCD religion class. I really loved it, and I was learning a lot about my faith. We started meeting couples and enjoyed being part of the parish. Eventually, we were approved for a baby, and the waiting began.

During the years of trying to have a baby nothing seemed to work. We found out both of us had problems, yet the doctors had hope. It was an emotional roller coaster, month after month. I would get hopeful, and each month my hopes would burst. It was a very difficult time for the both of us.

At one point, my doctor suggested that I have a laparoscopy to find out what was really going on inside of me. I did; it was around July 30, 1982. I remember the date, because my niece was born then, and my mother-in-law had to leave to be with her daughter who was having the baby. The doctor didn't find anything wrong with me. But as he was closing me up, they started to lose me. The doctor had nicked a main artery in my leg, and I was bleeding to death. He sewed up the artery, and it took a long six weeks to heal.

Finally, our patience was rewarded. Danah Maria was born July 6, 1982, in Mobile, Alabama. We were told about her in October. She was three months old, and we got her right around our seventh wedding anniversary.

We loved being parents. She was such an easy child. The first morning, I actually woke her up; it was eight in the morning, and she was still sleeping. I was worried something was wrong—she should have been awake I thought. She had gone down the night before at eight o'clock—twelve hours! She took two naps a day, for almost two hours each time, and she slept ten to twelve hours a night. This was an incredible first-mom experience. The extended family teased us about how easy she was.

Danah did not smile much and seemed a little too laid back. That changed after a few months, because we were always in her face and interacting with her. I remember lying on the floor by the sliding glass door with the sun shining through, talking to her and giggling. Dav was always talking to her too. She was the delight of our lives. The people at Dav's work did not even know her name for months, because he only referred to her as, "my baby girl." She went everywhere with us. At church, I could put her down on a blanket by the kneeler, and she would go to sleep.

In November of the next year, we were given Daniel Matthew. He was three weeks old. We had told our social worker we wanted another baby right away. They told us we had to wait a year before we even started the process again. When Danny was born, all of the couples who were approved and were waiting for a baby, wanted a girl. We were told Danny fit our family. It was the desire of the biological mother for her baby to have siblings and to be placed before Christmas—Danny had been born on November 18.

Danny was a sickly child. He was always crying and spitting up. When he was about three months old, we asked Dav's mother, Maw Maw Lou, to watch the kids for us. I needed a break. We drove the two hours to Biloxi on Friday to drop them off, and Maw Maw Lou would bring them back Sunday.

Early Saturday morning she called, saying, "Paw Paw said I had to ask you if I can change Danny's formula." She added, "I think he's allergic to it."

I didn't have a problem, and said, "Yeah, go right ahead."

When we got Danny back, he was a different child. I thank God for my mother-in-law, a very wise and wonderful lady. I have loved my in-laws from the beginning.

One Sunday at church, a priest came to visit our parish to talk about Marriage Encounter, a weekend away for couples. We each were holding a squirming child, and when the priest mentioned a weekend away, we looked at each other, shaking our heads. I was thinking, *If the church is involved, it must be okay.*

We went. On that weekend, we experienced a whole new way of communicating. One of the talks asked the question, "What do you hope to get from this weekend?" After we both wrote about it and exchanged notebooks, we were surprised to find that we both wanted a deeper relationship with God.

We had been approached previously by a couple at church to come to a prayer meeting. After the marriage encounter weekend, we decided to try it out. I have to say, I was very grateful for the friend who took us aside to explain a little about what would happen. They began by saying a prayer, and then they started singing, which was nice. After the song, they started praising God and speaking in words I did not understand. I felt uncomfortable. Next there was the raising of their hands; it was sign of freedom and confidence, which I wasn't comfortable with. We reluctantly stayed. When we left, we both commented how strange it was. Yet we felt we should go back—we felt there was something there.

We ended up going through a Life in the Spirit class, and we were prayed over for empowerment of the Holy Spirit. It was an incredible experience for both of us. The scriptures came alive for me. I could not get enough of the Bible. My husband also experienced a similar excitement for our faith. It was as if a light had come on; Mass became so awesome. The joy and peace of the power of the Holy Spirit was invigorating. I now understood that God's joy was a gift that no man could give or take away.

We were also asked to become part of the Marriage Encounter team, giving talks on the weekends. It was an awesome, growing time in our faith. We met some incredible holy couples, who were such blessings in our life. We did this for a total of about seven years. The more we served God and our religious community, the better our relationship was with one another.

CHAPTER 11

MOVING BACK TO BILOXI

When Danah and Danny were almost three and two, we moved back to Biloxi. Dav had gotten a job offer there out of the blue, and in our hearts, we had always wanted the kids to be around family more. It was a great time. My sister Lila had two girls who were close in age to our children. We did many things together.

We had the opportunity to go to Israel with a group. Dav's brother Anthony, who is a priest, put together the trip with a couple of his priest friends. My mother-in-law came too. It was a wonderful experience.

God is always teaching us though. Dav and I were two of the youngest in the group. We were about twenty-eight, and nearly everyone else was fifty-five-plus. As I edit this, I am now fifty-five-plus—how our perspective changes over time.

On the first day, we arrived at our hotel atop a hill next to the Sea of Galilee. Dav was the adventurous type, and he wanted to go down a steep hill to the water. He went ahead of me, but I was hesitant; he eventually coaxed me to come down. I started but realized I was picking up speed and could not stop myself. I was stopped by a four-foot boulder of coral, and I ended up lying across it. My shin below my knee was all scraped up, and I had a difficult time walking. Dav carried me on his back up the hill to the hotel.

Once we got to the hotel, another exciting adventure began. I needed to go to the hospital. Our tour guide put us in a taxi and spoke very fast to the taxi driver, and we sped off. I was more scared for my life on that taxi ride than I had ever experienced. He whipped around corners and squeezed in between cars as if there was an emergency. But the worst was yet to come.

The hospital was nothing like the ones in the States. I was on a bed with a curtain around me, and a pregnant nurse was walking around, smoking a cigarette and eating a dill pickle as she cared for the people. Being allergic to cigarette smoke, I was rapidly feeling worse than when I first came in. I did not have the breathing attack, but I was nauseous, and my head was pounding. A man had died in a bed near me, and the family was crying horribly.

Not understanding what anyone was saying was the worst. The doctor spoke very little English; he kept saying "toxoid shot," which we did not understand. But I needed to get one. We finally understood it was a tetanus shot, but getting a shot in a country I was not familiar with was scary. I had chipped part of my shin bone and cut my leg up, but thank God, there were no broken bones. Hours later, we were able to leave. And then I was as slow as everyone else. As always, God had taught me a valuable lesson. Change your attitude and slow down. I did and had an enjoyable, spirit-filled time.

Not long after we moved to Biloxi, I became pregnant. It was a difficult pregnancy, and I ended up losing the baby early on. I was extremely sick the entire time. I did not experience as great a loss as Dav did. He shared later how he had really wanted that baby. Losses are part of life, and later in my life, I did have to come to terms with the loss of that baby.

We became involved with a couples group in our parish and built great relationships. We started a child co-op at our church so parents could go to church and listen to the mass without the distraction of babies and toddlers. At one point, we had a young, pregnant, single woman live with us until she was able to get on her feet. Being involved with people and serving others ended up really helping us. We grew and learned so much from those relationships. Between our family and our church friends, life was abundantly full and blessed.

One day, when Danny was about three, we were at Dav's parents' house visiting. All of a sudden, I realized Danny was not in the house. My eye caught him through the sliding-glass door, halfway up the pool slide ladder. Before I realized it, I was pulling open the door and screaming, "Danny, get down from there."

As he started to hurriedly descend, he missed the step and fell, landing on his head. It was one of the most traumatic experiences I had as a young mom, and I ran and picked him up. He had a seizure, his body stiffing up and eyes rolling back, and then he went limp and would not respond.

Dav, Maw Maw Lou, and I got in the car and drove Danny to the hospital, which was only three minutes away. I remember praying to God to help him. At the hospital, he woke up after a little while and was fine, acting as if nothing had happened. They still wanted to take tests, and the tests showed that nothing was wrong.

From that experience, I learned not to scream when a child was in danger.

Danny was my challenger of excitement. That was only one of several occasions when God saved him—it just wasn't his time.

When Danny was around four, Dav was going for a run one Sunday afternoon. Danny asked if he could go, and Dav told him no, not this time. I was cooking on the grill and sitting on the swing enjoying the weather. All of a sudden, I thought, *Where are the kids?* They had been playing dress up. But it was too quiet, and Danny was a loud child.

I asked Danah where Danny was, but she didn't know. I ran around the house, calling for Danny, and then I remembered that he had wanted to go with his dad. I grabbed Danah and put her in the car, and we drove to the end of the street, which intersected a four-lane highway on the beach. The traffic was heavy, and I could not get across. I got out of the car and went into the middle of the highway to stop traffic, waving my arms wildly at cars and screaming for them to stop. They did. I ran back to my car and went across the highway. Not very far down the road, on the beach side, I saw Danny running back toward the direction of the house. I pulled over and ran up to him, grabbing him and holding him for what seemed forever.

He kept saying, "I want Daddy. I want Daddy." My heart was bursting with emotion, and I could barely breathe or move. Dav wore headphones when he ran, and he had not heard Danny calling him. As I think back to that day and wonder how Danny got across that highway, I know his guardian angel was with him; it wasn't his time nor had it been his time when he fell from the pool slide ladder.

When Dav got back from his run, Danny, Danah, and I were sitting on the swing outside.

Dav said to me, "What's wrong? You're as white as a ghost."

When I told him what had happened, he felt so bad; he never wore headphones again while running.

Our chicken was burnt to a crisp that day, as I had not turned off the grill when I left. But we could live with that fiasco.

CHAPTER 12

CHANGES

We were in Biloxi for three years. Dav's job was good, but he was offered a job back in Pensacola that was hard to pass up. The week before we were to leave, I threw myself on the bed, crying to Dav, "You can change this; they both want you. Let's stay." As always, Dav had good wisdom and knew this was what we were to do. There I was again, only thinking of myself. Was I ever going to mature?

At the time we were to leave, the housing market was not good in Biloxi. We had done many improvements to the house, and we thought we had put too much money in the house, and we would not get it back. When we were looking for a house in Pensacola, we decided to get a less expensive one, assuming we would not get as much as we wanted from the Biloxi house. If the house did not sell in Biloxi, his company would buy it, so we knew we would get a certain amount. We started looking in Pensacola for a house we could afford, based on what the company would give us.

We put our Biloxi house on the market for what we wanted, with the realtor saying that it was not a good idea. We got three offers in the course of a few days. The house sold for what we were asking.

The house in Pensacola was able to get a lot of extra special care since we had more money. We had the hardwood floors redone. Dav changed all the doors to solid wood with glass knobs, a dream of mine. We knocked out a wall and gutted the kitchen. I think we liked knocking out walls. It was November, and I was washing dishes outside in an ice chest. Thank God, it was Florida. It was the hardest room to remodel because we lived in our kitchen. I loved to cook, and eating out got old fast.

Then we decided to add an in-ground, concrete pool with a huge deck across the whole back of the house. We built the deck and a retaining wall around two sides of the pool. I am not sure how much I helped. Dav could hammer three nails to my one. But I remember him saying, "Keep going, Dor. You are helping." Those projects kept us busy for a couple of years.

During that time, we took in a seventeen-year-old, Valera, because her mother was moving back to Texas, and Valera wanted to finish her last year of school in Pensacola. We were friends with her sister and had met the family a few times. She was a great help to us, and we loved her. Valera was a blessing to the family. It's funny, I taught her how to drive and let her drive my Audi, yet when my own girls became of age, I paid someone else to teach them.

We had joined a great parish, the Cathedral of the Sacred Heart, which had an elementary school connected to the parish. It was three minutes from our home. Danah was able to go to a connecting school of the Sacred Heart called Morning Star for educable, challenged students who needed a little extra help. It was a wonderful school. She loved it. Danah was quiet and saw everything black or white. You either did the right thing or it was wrong—no in-between. She was our baby girl.

Danny was a higher-strung child. He was full of life and spoke his mind very loudly. There was something special about him though. The two of them were such joys in our life. God had blessed us abundantly. They were well-behaved and obedient for the most part.

We met many wonderful families through the school and parish. Dav was on the school board for a while, and I volunteered at the school often. The pastor of this parish had gone on a Marriage Encounter weekend that we helped present, so he knew a lot about us from our sharing on that weekend. He asked us to head up a couples group with couples he knew from different parishes. I thought that was odd at the time, because it's easier to form stronger relationships with people you might see at church or other functions. But we formed wonderful relationships with those couples, and some of them I still stay in touch with.

Life was exciting. We had bought a twenty-six-foot sailboat in Biloxi right before we left. Pensacola was a great place for a boat. Dav and my sister Lila's husband, Randy, sailed it from Biloxi to Pensacola one weekend. They had an exciting time. At one point, the weather was a bit stormy, and they ran aground; they had to wait it out till the tide rose again. It was a tense six or so hours. The boat was big enough for us to sleep on, which was always an adventure. We had many outings with friends and other families. The Navy has a Blue Angels air show over Pensacola Beach at different times of the year, and the pilots do some incredible maneuvers. That was always a great weekend on the boat for us. It brought back some of my childhood memories of just being on the water.

Chapter 13

Blending of Two Families

With the remodeling of the house about finished, I had time to think, and I started desiring more children. Life was just way too easy. I laugh today about that thought.

I told Dav I needed him to pray about this, because we both needed to want it to happen. Knowing how I could influence him with what I wanted, I thought it was too big for it to be only my idea. Maybe I'm finally starting to mature out of my selfishness. Little did I know how much more I really needed to grow.

I told Dav he needed to make the first move. A few months later, he came home and said I need to get a sitter two nights a week for six weeks. Dav had called Catholic Charities, and they said we already had two children, and they had a waiting list for parents with none. They suggested he call the state. He did, and they were starting a session for adoptive parents very soon. We attended the classes. We were not sure about some of the things we heard on the needs and caring for the children. We believed there needed to be boundaries and consequences. We felt that as long as Dav and I stayed united, the kids would feel our love and experience security. How to actually do that is different for everyone. We finished the classes and went to a session where we could look at albums of all the children waiting to be adopted. It was so overwhelming; we skimmed through one book, but we both felt that was not for us and we left. A few days later, a woman from the agency called. She said that she and a coworker felt from the moment they met us that a sibling group of three children might fit us: Christopher was six, Autumn had just turned five, and Holli was two and a half. She asked if we would be interested in looking at their portfolio.

I checked with Dav first, and we felt we should look into it. I went to the agency and read the very thick binders of each child. They had been placed in many foster homes within a short time, and the stories I read were incredible. My heart ached for them. I knew in my heart this was right. What was funny was that I wasn't scared by what I read. I felt love could change anything. I did not realize what the word *love* meant, but I have learned. To love to the max is what Jesus did for us; he experienced rejection, and he loved anyway. He was crucified, and he loved anyway so that we could be saved.

The three of them had the same mom. The two girls had an African American dad. The girls had beautiful, dark skin, and I still repent to them for not knowing how to work with their hair. Thank God, they figured it out.

Adopting biracial girls was a concern for us when we thought of our extended family. We were concerned for the girls and wanted to make sure they would be loved. The decision was made, and my husband commented that if the family members didn't accept them, it would be their loss. These children were loved, I thought at times even more than our original two, and it was great.

We were able to meet them on a few occasions, and then, all of a sudden, they were sleeping over for a long weekend. They were placed very quickly in our home—God's timing. We were told that things did not usually happen that fast. We knew this was what God wanted.

It was Easter of 1991, and God started purifying me and my husband. Our lives had changed. I remember going to the services for Good Friday and a deacon was singing some beautiful and moving hymns in the loft before Mass. Autumn said to me, "Is he an angel?" They were sponges, soaking up all that was new and exciting.

To jump from two extremely well-behaved eight- and seven-year-olds to five children overnight was, to say the least, incredible. We now had an eight-year-old, a seven-year-old, a six-year-old, a five-year-old, and a two-and-a-half-year-old. Thank God, we were young and excited about life and the adventures ahead. It became clear this was not going to be easy. But, God had placed a love in my heart for them with an attitude of "I won't ever give up; I'll keep going till I break." This kept me going, and prayer was the foundation for my strength.

At the time of the adoption, I was in college. I had gone before we adopted the two babies, and I did not go back until after they were in school. When we adopted the three, I was in school again and had six classes left to finish my two-year degree. I felt at the time that my vocation was to be a mom and wife. I let school go and decided to embrace motherhood wholeheartedly.

When we took the pre marriage classes from church before we got married, they had asked the question "How many children do you want?" My answer had been zero. I laugh at myself now.

Just having more children to manage was a workout, but on top of it were the habits and rejections that had influenced them in their formative years. I am a structured person and so I like order. We ate every meal together as a family. Bedtime was nonnegotiable. I remember once when Autumn did not like her bedtime, and she screamed for hours, throwing everything off her bed out into the hallway, even her sheets. We had had a priest and some couples over on that particular night, and they could not believe what they heard. I think back and realize that she could have come out of her room and yelled at us, but she did not. I think it had to do with the confidence Dav and I had with nonnegotiable situations. It reminded me of how I saw my own parents and how I learned what was expected of me—we kids instinctively knew the limits. As I look back, I remember experiencing protection from those boundaries.

Our family schedule included meal time, snack time, homework time, chore time, bath time, and bedtime; as you can see, I like structure. Some people have raised their eyebrows when they found out the kids were not even allowed to open the fridge or go in the pantry without permission. I had never had an issue with the two older ones going in the fridge or pantry without asking. I am talking about children who were younger than eight. The structure made life with so many children less stressful, yet it was still a lot of work. But I had learned to not be afraid of hard work as a child. My training and upbringing had prepared me for what God had for me now.

We were a family who loved the outdoors, and since we lived in Florida, the weather was conducive most of the year to being outside. In the summer, it was really too hot to camp, so we camped in the spring and fall. Summer was for being on the sailboat and at the beach. We would join other families at the beach for the whole day and go back to the house and swim in the pool.

We had an antenna for our television because we did not want to spend money on cable. We did not watch much TV anyway. We also didn't get the newspaper, partly because of the expense, and partly because we did not want the kids to spend hours reading the newspaper. We believed there was too much information for kids. We did, on occasion, get the Sunday paper and let the boys read the sports section, and we let them all read the cartoons.

Not long after we adopted the three, I noticed something that made another big change in our lives. On Saturday mornings, the children could get up quietly and go down to watch an hour or so of cartoons. I started to notice that the younger children could not refocus on the next step when the TV was shut off. Their behavior was uncooperative and filled with whining. Lent was approaching, and we had been wondering what we could do as a family. Their behavior inspired us to have no TV for quite some time.

Another thing I noticed was that the younger children did not know how to play: they needed to be entertained by someone or something. Our first two could play for hours using their imagination. It took the three youngest a while, but their cooperation became much better, and they learned how to play and use their imagination too. It was a lot of work on my part to introduce activities for them to choose from. The young ones also needed to learn that inside activities and outside activities were different. We eventually brought the TV back into the house but only for a Friday night movie night as a family with special snacks.

My husband even built something in the wall for the TV. A

large, framed picture hung from a hinge that covered the TV in the wall. The hinge allowed the picture to be lifted up and locked in place. None of the children could raise it and lock the picture in place.

Our lives had changed drastically. There was so much to learn. The challenges of raising these children drew me to my knees. I believe God placed an understanding in my heart of what they had missed in those formative years before our family. Yet their rejection toward me was real. These three children did not know how to respond to the good things happening to them. Celebrations, trips—anything that was a blessing—turned into turmoil; they could not handle good. It was as if they thrived on negativism and turmoil. I needed to stay very close to Jesus to receive comfort. I kept meditating on the cross and receiving my strength to go on from the knowledge that Jesus had experienced rejection, he had experienced suffering and pain. Uniting my cross to Jesus and not running from it gave me the strength I needed at the time.

Since they were three and four years old, the older children rarely had to be disciplined. They were loved and corrected with boundaries from the time they could crawl. The need for children to receive boundaries with love is essential in raising healthy, happy, well-balanced children. My experience with the three younger children was mind-boggling. At one point, I felt that I had tried everything and nothing had worked. It was as if they were afraid to have anything good happen to them.

One night, we were meeting with our couples group, and I shared my frustration of nothing working with these three children. One woman asked, matter-of-factly, "Have you prayed over them?"

I was dumbfounded; why had I not thought of that? Where had

we been? Sometimes, when you are in the forest, you cannot see the trees. I had been engulfed with daily, often hourly, crises, and I could not see beyond the trees.

I believe that is why it is so important to have relationships with others, with friends who are striving for holiness, desiring to do God's will. That night, after everyone left, Dav and I went into each room and prayed over each child. Years before, we had been part of the charismatic movement, and we were familiar with praying over people, but we were not part of an active prayer group at the time. As we prayed over each sleeping child individually, the two older children slept peacefully. The three younger ones jerked and moved. When the first child did this, I remember thinking, with a little fear, *What is this?* My husband started praying stronger, and I followed his lead. The next night, we used holy water as we prayed. All of the children were asleep. The two older ones remained peaceful again. The other three were jerking and moving. We did this each night for a while, and the jerking finally stopped. That actually started a ritual of laying hands on the children before they went to bed and blessing them. I did notice a change, but they had so much baggage. We had to just keep praying. God showed me their goodness and kept telling me to love them through it. God was really in charge. Dav and I were drawn closer to each other with God for strength in the battles.

CHAPTER 14

FAMILY MEMORIES

Dav and I felt that we needed to make memories fast. With the other two children, we had made albums of all sorts of vacations and visits with the family in Biloxi. So we began a quest to take mini trips often, taking many pictures and putting together family albums with captions. What fun!

The year before we adopted the three, we had been saving for a trip to go to Disney World and stay inside Magic Kingdom. That trip had to be adjusted. We could not spend the money for three more children, and we knew we needed another adult or two with us for help. A friend had heard about the Disney World trip and said, "Oh, you can use our timeshare and only pay the small transfer fee." Our sister-in-law to be, Karen, and her friend Julie came along and helped us out. We had a few moments, but all in all, it was a good trip. The ratio of four adults to five kids was a great blessing.

Memories began: camping trips, sleeping on our sailboat trips, going to the beach often, and visiting family in Biloxi.

Once we went on the boat for the weekend, and Valera came with us. After we were all settled down and it was getting dark, we put the kids to bed. Dav and I got in the dingy and went to the shore to try to catch crabs; there were not any crabs but there were shrimp. We walked along the shore in knee-deep water with the lantern and the small nets we had brought. It was a great evening. We caught enough for everyone to have a fried shrimp sandwich the next day for lunch. Great times, great memories.

One of the issues with the younger kids was that they had a hard time ending a trip. I suppose part of it was that things changed again. When we would leave Biloxi, they would cry almost all the way home, because they did not want to leave. Visiting the family was always a fun time, but real life was real life.

CHAPTER 15

HOUSE ADDITION

Not long after the adoption, we decided to add onto our already large four-bedroom home. We enlarged our bedroom with a sitting area and a bigger bathroom, added two more bedrooms and a large bath, and put a three-car garage underneath. The single-car garage was to become my art room/laundry room.

Dav drew up the plans and started the groundwork. We had a circular driveway put in. The kids loved riding their bikes on it. Dav had a few friends help with the heavier work, and he hired someone to work on the roof. It was exciting for the kids. The boys created many things with the extra wood, and the girls loved gathering the sawdust and pretending to cook with it and make things. At times, the kids had a chance to hammer nails.

We were super busy and loving life. We were involved with the kids, school, and church. We had good friends who we spent vacations and weekends with. And we made frequent trips to visit family and friends in Biloxi, where there was always a celebration happening.

With all of our life commitments, our home-addition project took four years to complete.

CHAPTER 16

BABY SURPRISE

It was in the third year of the project that I miraculously became pregnant. I suppose I was preoccupied enough finally, but in reality, God had the best plan. I was thirty-eight, and I remember thinking that I was too old for a baby—our youngest had just started kindergarten.

My husband was ecstatic. When we told the kids, Danny, then nine, jumped up crying, "No we don't need another one," and he ran to his room.

Dav and I were taken aback. When we talked to him, he said, "You don't have enough time for me now. I have to share everything." We had made the two older kids share all their toys, and the three younger ones did not know how to take care of things. Many of the toys were broken. Danny was having a hard time.

Things settled down after the shock of the news wore off. The house had an excitement of expectation. I loved being pregnant; I felt the healthiest I had been in a while. I really love chocolate, but during my pregnancy, I had no desire to eat it. I wanted fruit and vegetables.

We had just bought a new van that had seven seats. With the new arrival coming, the van was not going to be big enough. When we started looking, the salesman showed us a fifteen-passenger van. I was intimidated by that huge vehicle. I did not want to even drive it. But Dav encouraged me, and I did. It did take time, but I became comfortable driving the monster. I remember Dav saying, "Let's see if God fills this van." I was worried.

I found out I was pregnant when I was three months along. Four months later, I was in the hospital dying from toxemia. They gave me a shot to help the babies lungs develop. The doctors were trying to hold off as long as they could for the baby to grow just a little bit bigger. After four or five days, they had to do an emergency C-section. The baby boy came out breathing on his own. He was fine, just small—4.4 pounds. God's miracle. I, on the other hand, did not get well so fast. Normally, once you have the baby, the toxemia goes away. The toxemia stayed with me longer, and I had other complications.

The baby did not get a name for a few days. I remember Dav sitting by my bed. I was sort of out of it. He was saying, "We have to decide on a name." He had a Bible, and he started naming names. "Joshua" felt right, and I wanted to use "Mark" from my younger brother. So Joshua Mark was named.

I came home first, and Josh followed almost a week later. Dav would go to the hospital two or three times a day, and with work and the children, he had his hands full. I was so sick, I only got to see Josh once in the hospital. He looked so helpless with all of those tubes in him. It was such an emotional helplessness. I could hardly stand it. I wanted to scoop him in my arms and not let go. I broke down crying, and they took me to another room.

After Josh came home, life was even harder. It was a six-week recovery, but for the first four weeks I didn't even get out of bed much. I did get to finally hold him at home, but that was about all I could do. The brunt of everything was on Dav. He was incredible. One night, he was kneeling next to the bed, looking exhausted with dark circles under his eyes. He was concerned about me and asking what he could do for me. Dav loved us all with unconditional love. He just kept giving of himself with a peace and joy that you wanted to be around.

I could hear him in the mornings, getting the kids ready for school with his joyful self. He had a corny sense of humor sometimes. If one of the kids hurt themselves (not to bad) he would say in a serious voice, "Do *dhat* again, I missed it," and then he would start tickling them. It's amazing how that helped break the tension.

Preparing for dinner was always a challenge during the week. There could be chaos and arguing going on, yet once Dav walked in the house, it seemed to disappear. He just had a peace and joy about him.

Thank God for our church family. They fed us for quite a while and helped as much as they could with the children. We finally got through that time of ill health. Josh was baptized on April 10, two months after he was born. It was not until then that I began to really engage in running the house again.

At the same time, in Biloxi, my older sister, Lila was in a terrible accident. She was walking on the sidewalk on her way to work, and a huge truck turned the corner. A utility pole sticking out of the back hit her from behind and threw her across the road.

She should have died, but she didn't, although she had a very long recovery. I missed her not being part of my life at that time, and me not being part of hers. I believe our faith helped us to offer up our own sufferings for the other. We were bonded through Christ.

CHAPTER 17

DAY-TO-DAY LIFE HAPPENINGS

A turning point for me was realizing what a great man Dav was and seeing his suffering and sacrifice for us. He loved, and he did it with great ease. I hate to admit it, but I was a controller, and I made sure everyone knew what was on my mind. I usually got whatever I wanted. Dav was a joyful, easy-going guy who knew how to love.

One time, when he was working outside on the house, Danny, then ten years old, asked him to fix his bike. I was bringing Dav coffee and a snack. I saw him fixing the bike, and I was a little upset. We had five kids at the time. When Dav was working on the house, I always told the kids, "Leave Dad alone; he's busy." Yet as I look back on that scene, I see that he had his priorities right. If he did get aggravated about being interrupted, you never knew it.

Dav had a ritual when he and the kids finished cleaning the yard. He would bring them all to the 7-Eleven store and let them chose a soda. It was a really big deal because we rarely had sodas in the house. The kids always enjoyed cleaning the yard for that soda.

Right before Christmas, Dav would tell the kids we had to spruce up the yard for Santa's reindeer to land. What excitement they shared that day as they raked and cleaned the backyard.

One Sunday, after lunch, Dav went downstairs to watch a football game, and the five kids followed him. I was left in the kitchen to clean up. I was not happy; we all usually cleaned up together. I went downstairs and huffed about doing the kitchen by myself.

Dav responded, "We'll all do it later, come on."

Oh no, it needed to be done right then. My emotional self-had come out, and I huffed out of the house and drove off to think. The children told me much later that they had been worried. But when they looked at Dad sitting on the couch, he kicked his legs out, crossed them at the feet, put his hands behind his head while looking at the TV, and said, "She'll be back," with great confidence. The kids felt relieved because he wasn't worried. And, of course, I did come back—and with a better attitude.

I have a funny story about the kids that we call, The Spaghetti Dinner. When I brought the children to school, they each had a day to sit in the front seat. This was a big deal. There were five children and five school days. Simple, right? The rule was that the day you got to sit in the front seat, you were the one to set the table for dinner, before five o'clock. The children never forgot what day they got to sit in the front seat. But one child had a harder time remembering to set the table. The problem was, when I would remind that child, he would respond with whining and complaining, saying that I was interrupting his playtime. I didn't mind reminding the children, but when he would say things like I was interrupting his play time, it rubbed me the wrong way. One day, it was the whining child's turn. Dav was away on a business trip for the week, and I was tired and did not want to get into another argument or listen to the complaining. I felt something needed to change, and I had an idea. I called the children downstairs to dinner and placed noodles directly onto the table at each spot. Then I proceed to add the sauce on top

The children came in, and when they realized what I was doing they started in on the child who was supposed to set the table that day, saying in very strong voices, "You did not set the table." I was as cool as a cucumber. Then one of them realized that another child was to have washed the table after breakfast, and that child had not done a very good job. So they were yelling at that child about not washing the table very good after breakfast. It was a sight to behold and listen to. When they were finally sitting down, I started to go around the table with the gallon of milk, asking if they would like some milk, and getting ready to pour it on top of their spaghetti. Each one was screaming, "No, no, no." I sat down and started the prayer. I was the only one with a fork, a plate, and a glass.

By now, they had all calmed down and one asked, "Do we really have to eat off the table?"

I responded, "Yes, and all of it."

Another question was, "Without a fork?"

I respond, "Yes."

One child could not stand for her hands to be dirty. She didn't want to touch the food.

I believe this was the inspiration of the Holy Spirit and not of me. My action was to the point and related to the situation, and I was too peaceful—not like me at all.

As I had their full attention, I reminded them, "We have a rule that the person who gets to sit in the front seat of the van sets the table for dinner. None of you ever forgets to sit in the front seat on your day, so why would you forget to set the table by five o'clock on that day too? You are always hungry before dinner, so food is on your mind."

The truth was, it was mostly the attitude of the one particular child. I also told them, "We are a family, and what one person does affects the rest. We are all accountable to one another. We all experience consequences of our actions. The ripple effect of one's consequences affects others—the good and the bad."

As I was writing this story, it made me think of how Jesus was the prime example of this. He came to earth and became man. God the creator, became man to save us. He died for our sins; he suffered for our sins. He loved us first, even when he knew what we would do. The ripple effect of our sins crucified Christ. That is a powerful love. We are called to love like Christ loved.

I sat there with great serenity and ate, and not one child left the table without eating what was set before him or her.

On the following days, the children reminded one another before the five o'clock time limit that it was time to set the table. I had no more issues with that particular area of chores.

This story has become a classic in our family, which the children love to retell and laugh about. Recently, at my daughter's wedding, one of her friends who has a couple of children approached me and said, "I want to hear the spaghetti story from the source." I retold the story, and she thought it was the coolest, to-the-point correction she had ever heard. I suppose it could have backfired if the children were too young, but it worked for me at the time. Praise God.

CHAPTER 18

A SUMMER TO REMEMBER

In the summer of 1995, Dav decided we should take a big trip and explore the north. I was not as eager. We had a sixteen-month-old, an almost-seven-year-old, and nine-, ten-, eleven-, and twelve-year-olds. We did have a fifteen-passenger van, but for a three-week trip, I was not too thrilled at the idea. But my husband's excitement became contagious. This was going to be a great adventure.

The plan unfolded. We would go to Atlanta first and see Coca-Cola World and then head up toward Washington, DC, to tour the city with a priest friend for a day. I liked to dress the kids in matching outfits or something that made them stand out. That day in Washington, all the children had on bright, rainbow-colored, tie-dyed T-shirts. I bought a larger shirt for Holli, altered it, and made a shirt for Josh out of the extra. A man on the street yelled out to us, "Here comes the rainbow family." That was a fun day.

After Washington, we went to New Jersey. A few years before, a group of religious brothers called the Brotherhood of Hope came to work in our church from New Jersey. We became friends with them over time, and we met some of their families in New Jersey. We stayed with one of those families for a few days. They brought us on the ferry to the Statue of Liberty and Ellis Island, which were exciting adventures for the kids. Afterward, we headed out and stopped to camp for a week at the Shenandoah National Forest. That was beautiful. Then we headed on toward Stone Mountain in Georgia and camped some more. The laser light show on the mountain was incredible.

It was a vacation to remember. My job was to keep Dav nourished and hydrated, because he did all the driving, which was what he preferred. Keeping order with the six children for hours on end was my other job. I had put together a bag for each child, filled with things to keep that child occupied. But I also put together a few other bags to interchange items at different times of the trip, hoping to keep them entertained. We had two Walkman's that they took turns with, which had stories to listen to and some music. Between the exciting snack times and activities, it went pretty well. We would play the quiet game when it got too noisy. They were very good, except Josh, who really did not understand yet how to play the game. He would say, "I done," and we would all laugh. But he took good naps, which was a blessing. The boys loved Legos, and they had a big seat all to themselves in the back. The girls had their dolls and loved books and drawing and coloring. Once I turned around, and Holli had her doll's blanket wrapped around her head, and she was holding her baby, feeding it. She looked so cute talking to her baby and pretending. We played the alphabet game and the number game. Our camping days were the most relaxing, as we were able to stay put for the week and not have an agenda. We saw a bear and deer, which the kids had not seen in the wild before. In New Jersey, deer lived in people's yards and ate everything. We had an incredible three weeks exploring the north.

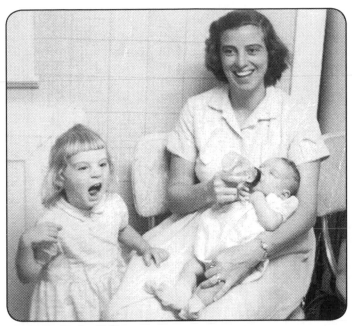

Lila, my mom Rita holding me (Dorea) in moms' arms.

Left to right, my sister Lila, Grandma Rita, my sister Kathy,
Mom, my brother Mark in Dad's arms and me (Dorea).

Me (Dorea), center holding brother Mark, sister
Kathy to right of Mark and cousins.

Left to right, me (Dorea) on my First Holy Communion,
my sister Kathy and my brother Mark.

1973, first year dating
Dav and me

Dav's brother's wedding 1974

Our wedding day October 18, 1975
my parents Clyde and Rita Ross

Dav's college graduation 1978

Working on the house we had built.

My parents and siblings as adults. Left to right, Ricky,
Kathy, Dad, Mom, Lila, on floor myself and Tina.

Dav with his parents and siblings as adults. Center
Mom (Lou Ella), top left to right, Dad (Ivon),
Anthony, Teresa, bottom Dav, Michael and Paul

Family photo 1986, Daniel 3, Danah 4

Our first family photo as a family of seven. Left to right, Christopher, Daniel, Holli, Danah and Autumn.

Dav with his other baby girl, the 26 ft. sailboat.

One of our many adventures on the baby
girl. Dav, Chris, Holli and Autumn.

Holli's first birthday with us. She is three. Left to right,
Christopher, Daniel, Holli, Autumn and Danah.

Five cute bikers, left to right, Holli, Autumn,
Christopher, Daniel, Danah

Our first Christmas tree hunt with five kids. Holli,
Christopher, Daniel, Danah and Autumn

Dav and Holli having a special moment.

Dav and Autumn, the kids loved hanging on Dav.

Our first big memory trip to Disney World. Left to
right, Holli and Daniel, Autumn and Chris, Karen
and Julie our incredible helpers, Danah and I.

Our first beach house vacation with five kids.

Our trip to the Smokey Mountains with three other families. Fifteen kids and eight adults.

Daniel leading the pack of tubers in the Smokey Mountains.

Our house before construction. 1991

After construction of our house in 1994.

Christmas 1993 Pregnant with Josh.

Dav and Josh home finally February 1994.

April 1994, Josh's baptism, family from Mississippi come to celebrate. Left to right top, Karen, Paul, Jorrie, Daniel, Stephanie, Danah, bottom left to right, Dav, Autumn, Me, Holli, Christopher, Sandi and Josh, Lila and Randy.

Josh and Autumn with Dav

Setting out on our three week adventure exploring
the north, summer of 1995. Me, Josh, Holli,
Daniel, Danah, Autumn, Christopher

Washington D.C. left to right, Christopher, Josh and
Dav, Autumn, Danah, Daniel, Holli and me

Loretta showing Josh the fish in the pond. Loretta was my angel from heaven who took care of the children while I was away with Daniel.

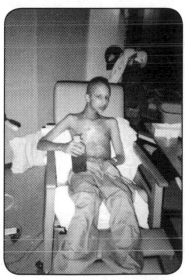

Daniel recovering from bone marrow transplant.

Summer of 1996, left to right, Autumn, Christopher,
Danah, me and Josh, Daniel, Holli.

Daniel's Make a Wish miracle in Hawaii.

Fr. Mike and Daniel in front of Notre-Dame Facade in France.

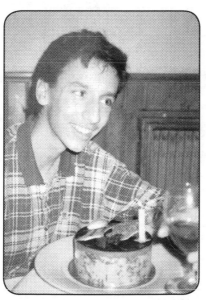

Daniel's last birthday, 14, in France, while
celebrating with a glass of wine.

January 1998, our last family photo with Daniel.

Daniel's art work, done in 1996, 1997, 1998.

2009 Autumn's wedding rehearsal dinner.
top left to right, Autumn, Anthony, Teresa, Robbin,
Paul, Aaron, Danah, Josh, John, bottom left to right,
me, Lila, Ginny, Azlyn, Jorrie, Karen, Holli.

Daughter Holli, nieces Gabby and Azlyn, daughter
Danah. Autumn's wedding rehearsal dinner.

Autumn's wedding 2009. Siblings, left to
right, Holli, Josh, Autumn, Danah.

My sister Lila and Autumn. Before Autumn's wedding.

Autumn and Mom 2009.

Summer of 2009 with siblings on Biloxi beach. Left to right bottom, Ricky, Lila, top left to right, Tina and me.

One of my art shows.

2011 family picture left to right, Holli, Josh, me, Danah holding
Camilla, Jeremy and Autumn with Thomas on the way.

Nana (me) holding Thomas Patrick my grandson. 2012

2012 Christmas, Danah, Josh and me.

CHAPTER 19

GRIEF BEYOND GRIEF

The construction on the inside of the house was finally finished. The four-year project was coming to a close. Dav had finished the front, the porch, and both sides of the house, which were twenty feet high or more. We still had the back of the house to complete. There were cedar shingles around part of the house, and we decided to remove them and put up vinyl. Dav rented the scaffolding, and everything was set.

This is how I remember that day. It was a beautiful January day—to be exact, January 14, 1996. The weather was slightly crisp; all we needed was a sweatshirt. I was making two huge, front-door wreaths, and some of the children were outside playing. Dav was ripping the shingles off the back of the house, getting it ready for the new siding.

I remember saying to Dav, "Shouldn't you wait and do that part after you put the porch roof on, then you could stand on the roof?" It looked a little scary to me. His response was an "Oh Dor", and he kept working. I always had an opinion and usually spoke it.

I was reminded that he had already finished the sides of the house, and that had been much higher. Danny had just finished picking up all the nails on the concrete next to the pool pump house, and he was getting on the scaffolding with Dav. I had gone into the garage to switch the laundry. Then I heard crashing and Danny screaming.

I ran out, and Dav was on the concrete, bleeding—not moving or really breathing. I knelt down beside him and remember screaming, "No, God! No! No!"

I touched him, and I was screaming at him, "Dav, can you hear me?" I saw blood coming from his mouth and nose, and he gave a gasp of one breath and then no more.

I was thinking, *This is not happening; this can't be happening.* After realizing that he wasn't responding, I left and ran to the neighbors, trying to get help. I must have been hysterical at the first neighbor's, but for some reason I left there and went to another house and another, but those two neighbors were not home. I remember, at one point, not knowing what to do. I just stood there in a daze, looking around and then staring at my hands that had blood on them. Then I ran back to the house.

When I returned, one of the neighbors was trying to resuscitate Dav. Then the rescue squad arrived and took over. Danny had called 911. The other children were not there when I returned. They told me later that they ran to a friend's home, which was a few blocks away. Josh was at the first neighbors' house I went to. While the rescue squad was there, I called my father-in-law and mostly just kept saying, "It's bad, it's bad. You need to come."

My brother-in-law Paul called me back, but I just kept saying, "It's bad, it's bad. Dav fell; you need to come."

I was in no shape to even explain what had happened. He had jumped from the bathhouse roof to the scaffolding, and the boards flipped. It was only about ten feet high, but he landed wrong.

The first night, I stayed at the hospital; I wouldn't leave. They made me take a pill to help me sleep. What little sleep I did get was on the floor.

The next day, I remember going home around Josh's bedtime to put him to bed, trying to keep things somewhat on a routine. His ritual for bedtime was that I would hold him in his room and sway back and forth singing "Alleluia," and he would always sing with me. I needed to keep that ritual of putting him to bed as much for me as for him. But then I went back to the hospital. Everything was such a blur, and it still is such a horrible pain to relive at times. Right now, as I write this, and every time I have had to reread this as I have worked on this book, I experienced a tightness and overwhelming fullness in my chest, which seems as if it's going to explode. Tears flowing down my face, and I need to keep taking deep breaths till the emotions pass. Repeating under my breath, Dear Jesus help me.....

The doctor said Dav had fallen directly on his head. The days after his fall just passed, and I have very little recollection of what I did. As I look back I needed those days to adjust to what had happened. I was numb; I could not even really cry.

On the fifth day, January 19, they told me he was officially brain dead. A priest friend, Father Mike, was with me, and he was talking, but I don't remember anything he said. I could not really comprehend the news. I wanted to scream, but I couldn't. I felt as if I had nothing left—nothing.

Even Josh, the cute, joyful, little toddler, couldn't pull me out of it. I kept thinking, *I can't do this, raise these kids by myself; I can't.*

It was true; I could not do it. But with God, all things are possible. I didn't fully know that yet.

As I was sitting in the room with Father Mike, after just hearing this news of Dav, the door opened and there stood three of my girlfriends. When I looked up and saw them, I yelled out, "Go away; you still have your husbands." They ran to me and held me, and we all cried and cried and cried for the longest time. Grief beyond grief. He wasn't just my husband he was my best friend.

When the family—Dav's brother Paul, and his wife Karen, and Dav's sister Teresa—and I were able to go in for the last visit, I remember thinking, *He is not really there. He is not really there.* The pain of just remembering that, even at this moment, years later, is excruciating. What I have learned over these years is when I have tried to ignore it or stuff it away my emotions control me. When I embrace them and ask God to help me I am given peace. Because of my faith, I am able to unite my suffering to the cross with Jesus, and I always experience peace.

In the hospital, they had Dav lying on a bed of ice, which never made any sense to me. He was so cold that his body actually shivered. I did not want to remember him like that, and I did not stay long. His siblings stayed longer. I made the decision to not let the children see him in the hospital. I am not 100 percent sure I did the right thing. But that is where I was at the time.

The wake and funeral were nothing I had ever experienced in my life. For hours, I stood and greeted people; certain people made me cry as I hugged them, and from others, I experienced a comfort of peace. There were many priests on the altar for the Mass. It was such a gift—even our bishop came. It was an incredible tribute to my husband; hundreds of people came to the wake and funeral.

The next few weeks were a total blur. I don't remember taking care of the kids or doing much of anything. I know that my friends and church family and our family from Biloxi were around a lot. I mostly remember being curled up in fetal position and crying for hours on end until I wanted to throw up. Yet life had to keep going.

Josh's second birthday was only a few weeks away. Josh's godparents, Toni and Jeff, had his birthday at their house. I don't remember much of that day, but we have a picture of him in a highchair with a cake in front of him. I do remember sitting there at the table, watching everyone doing something, but I had no energy or desire to be part of it. It was as if I was in my own little world of pain, just watching everything around me and being in a daze.

About a month after Josh's birthday, I took a video of Josh while the kids were at school. We were in the living room, and he was on the couch and had a book. The sun was beaming through the windows from behind him; it was a beautiful day. I asked him to sing for me, and he started singing "Alleluia," our special song that I sang to him anytime I put him to bed. It was so cute. I was asking him how old he was and other questions. All of a sudden, he put his arms out and started opening and closing his hand, saying, *"Daddy, Daddy, cm ear."*

It was as if he was looking at something or someone in the sunlight. As I watched, I remembered feeling I had to stay strong, and I asked, "What, Josh?" even though I knew what he said. He repeated it, and then he stood on the couch and looked out the window and kept saying, "Daddy, Daddy." This was where he would be most days waiting for his daddy to come from work, looking out the window.

I needed to change the subject, I was beginning to feel like I was unraveling. This was so painful to see Josh wanting his dad and it never happening. I wanted his dad so much too. I asked in a calming, soothing voice if he wanted to read his book for me, and we lost the moment.

Recently, the kids were watching the video, and I happened to walk by when that part of the video was playing. Josh, who was fifteen, asked, "How could your voice sound so unemotional."

I responded with a laugh, "I had to be strong and in control on the outside, but I was dying on the inside." I slapped his back and walked away and went to my room. I gathered my stuff and went to take a shower. In the shower, I fell apart, crying, finally, for that baby who wanted his daddy, for the fact that I could not change that, and for all of the rest of the emotions I could not release years ago. Even though I had cried in a fetal position many times, I did not do that when the kids were around. I felt I had to be strong for the kids. That was not the time to fall apart. I remembered the ice chest of shrimp I was helping my dad carry across that makeshift pier when I fell in. I had had the same feelings: No time to make a scene. Get the job done.

The kids had been an incredible challenge. I felt I had to have a fortress built around me to stay standing. They took turns every day and some days all day long with their emotional outbursts. Prayer and the Eucharist were my saving grace.

Even when I went back to my room after that shower, I continued crying into my pillow. Then I offered that suffering and pain up to God and experienced an incredible peace. When I went downstairs, Josh was alone. I was able to share my experience of that video and how inside of me was this deep seeded pain of seeing him want his dad so much and I wanted it too. It was a healing moment for me, and I think it was good for Josh to hear where I was coming from. Thanks be to God.

After the accident, I wouldn't go in the backyard. I remember standing in the living room, staring out into the backyard through the sliding glass doors, feeling almost paralyzed and thinking, *I will never go back out there again.* I had so many fun and wonderful memories, yet that one incident put total fear in me. The pain I now associated with the backyard was overwhelming. When Dav had gone away on business trips for a week or so, I would be left home to hold down the fort, so to speak. It was hard at times, yet I knew he was coming home. It was as if he was present invisibly. But after his death, I felt totally alone and abandoned. He wasn't even present invisibly. Yet I knew, deep down inside, God was there.

One morning, after I dropped the kids off at school and Josh at his morning daycare, I walked into the house and saw through the sliding glass door that the pool was half empty and water was spraying all over the place. We had had a slight freeze the night before, and it was warmer now. A pipe had burst. Not thinking, I ran outside to turn the valves off to stop the water. When I was finished, I realized I was standing in the area where Dav had fallen. I threw myself on the ground and wept bitterly for a very long time. The overwhelming pain was so intense that it was hard to breathe at times. After that experience, I was able to go out in the backyard again. A healing had begun.

I started doing unusual things to relieve the stress in my life. At the time, I had no idea that's what I was doing. I'd go jump on the trampoline by myself and jump so hard and fast, I would fall down exhausted and just lay there, crying. I also would swim laps until I couldn't go anymore. That one bothered me some, because I was alone outside—it was usually late at night or when the kids weren't home—and I knew in my head that water could be dangerous.

Our family and friends in Biloxi wanted to have a repast for

Dav about a month after his death. There were many people who could not come to Pensacola for the services. We went to Mass first and then to a reception. When I walked into the reception hall, someone was smoking. They forgot to put up little signs on the tables saying No Smoking. I gasped for air and was on the floor. It was a horrible experience. Much later, the children told me how they remembered that day. They were already experiencing an emotional upheaval, thinking I would not be able to take care of all of them, and wondering if they were all going to have to live with different relatives. They had seen me have one of those attacks at a restaurant a couple of years before. I had walked into the bathroom and someone was smoking, and I literally hit the floor and stopped breathing. Seeing it happen again at the repast made them think I was going to die too. Their stability was being shaken to the core.

I was brought to my father-in-law's home. Once I was alone and feeling a bit better, I remember crying and yelling at Dav for leaving me with all the kids and no one to take care of me with my problem. I was telling him that I could not do it, and I was yelling at God, too. The next time I walked into a situation where someone was smoking, I no longer had an attack. That was in 1996. Later, the smoke still bothered me, and I would still deal with headaches, but I no longer had the horrible breathing attacks. God had healed me. Thanks be to God.

CHAPTER 20

CHILDREN'S REMEMBRANCE

The children had their own remembrances of Dav's accident. Danah was sitting at the picnic table, making sand art. She says she saw two angels next to Dad, and when he jumped, they disappeared, and he fell. I believe her because of who she is and her innocence.

Danny shared that dad had told him to pick up the nails and pieces of wood off the concrete first. Danny had wanted to get on the scaffolding first, and he was not happy to do that job, but he did it. Finally, Danny got to go up on the scaffolding. Dad went to jump from the bathhouse roof to the scaffolding, and the boards on the scaffolding flipped. Dad started falling, and Danny tried to reach out to grab him. Dad pushed him back to the wall and said no. Dad fell on the concrete that Danny had just finished cleaning up.

Chris was in his room doing homework. He said he had had a fight with his dad about not doing his homework the day before. For a long time, Chris felt it was his fault because of the fight. When he heard the screaming, he ran outside and saw Dad on the concrete bleeding. He ran back inside to get an ice pack, and when he came back out, he realized that it was not going to help.

Autumn was playing with Josh on the swing set. She remembers grabbing Josh and running to where dad fell. Standing there not knowing what to do. When the neighbor came over they took Josh to their house.

Holli was at her First Holy Communion meeting. Someone went and got her from church and brought her home. She says that all she remembers of that day was seeing her dad's shoes as they were putting him in the ambulance. She had been told to stay in the car.

It is amazing the impact we all experienced that day, but each of us experienced something different.

Holli had always resented the fact that she was not there that day.

Years later, she saw clearly that God's plan was the best plan. It happened when she was babysitting an almost-two-year-old at our house for the weekend. I knew the family and the child, and it was not a big deal. On Sunday afternoon, the child had a seizure. That was such a traumatic experience for Holli. It was crazy. I was yelling for them to go get a neighbor. Josh left and started knocking on neighbors' doors trying to find someone home. Holli called 911. A friend of mine came and stayed with me, and we waited for the paramedics to come. We did a lot of praying. The little boy's grandmother lived down the street, and she came and went to the hospital with him. His parents had been on their way back and would be home in a couple of hours.

After everyone left, the kids and I looked at each other, and we all sat down in the living room. I commented, "So how do we just go on with our lives after experiencing that?" I suggested that we say the rosary, and we did. Afterward, we all shared our experience. Danah says that it reminded her of when Dad fell. I agreed; there were very similar emotions of helplessness and the unknown. I remember thinking, *Oh God, don't let him die; he can't die, not here.* Josh just said that it was weird. He had run up and down the street a few times trying to find someone home. At one house, my friend was not home, but her eighty-nine-year-old mother was. She didn't see well or hear well, and it took forever for her to tell Josh that her daughter wasn't home. He said he was about to burst inside, but he knew he had to stay calm with her. Holli was the most affected. She cried a lot and then made the comment that God had spared her from seeing what happened to Dad. I just held her, and we cried. It was hard to continue with regular life that day. Yet I believe we all grew, and healing did take place.

CHAPTER 21

WAKE-UP CALL

This adventure of walking on water became even more adventurous. Within six weeks after my husband's accident, I literally woke up.

It was three in the morning, and I heard water running. I got up and found my son Danny getting into the tub.

I asked in puzzlement, "What are you doing?"

He responded, "Mom, I told you my leg hurts; this is the only thing that helps the pain."

I went back to my bed in a daze. I didn't remember him telling me his leg hurt. But as I lay there, I felt in my heart, *You have to take care of this child.*

The next morning, I called the doctor, and we were able to see him that day. But both the doctor and I felt that the trauma of Dav's fall and Danny being on the scaffolding with him was why he was experiencing the pain. The doctor suggested just giving him Tylenol.

After a few days, I noticed Danny was starting to live only for the Tylenol. I called the doctor back with my concern, and he suggested that I only give it to him at night. When Danny heard this, he started screaming, "You can't do this to me; I can't stand the pain." I didn't budge in the decision made. He was obedient and did not complain anymore about the decision. A couple of days later, in the middle of the day, he was screaming for me to come. He was in the tub again, and he found a big lump on his leg. I vividly remember that day and how I called the doctor back and we got to go in immediately. He took some X-rays.

Later that day, the doctor's office called to have me come in for a consultation the following morning. I really do not know where my head was; I had no thought of it being serious. That next morning, I also had an appointment for my first grief-counseling session, which also turned into my last session. After the session, I dropped by the church office and visited with the pastor. I happened to mention that I was going to a consultation with the pediatrician. The pastor wouldn't take no for an answer and drove me there. I thank God for having him there.

The doctor told me Danny had cancer, and they set up appointments for Danny in three days at Shands Hospital in Gainesville, Florida, six hours away. I felt I was being whisked into a hurricane and had no control over anything. Sometimes I did feel the craziness, but at other times, I was oblivious to the craziness around me. Only God could do that.

I believe from that moment on, I experienced being carried by God, and he took care of all the details of my life. I may have not seen it as clear at the time, but as I look back, it is very evident.

Friends took care of the kids, and we were off to Gainesville.

On that first trip to Gainesville, God had an angel waiting for us. Father Mike, the pastor at our church, had a college friend, Wayne, who lived in Gainesville. He had us stay with him those three or four days during the test. Wayne lived less than five minutes from the hospital. He was a precious gift that God gave us. Wayne rode us around that first afternoon and showed me how to get to the hospital for the next day.

Danny was diagnosed with Ewing's sarcoma, a bone cancer, in March of 1996. A plan was made, and we were to come every three to four weeks on a regular cycle. We would go for about a week, and Danny would get rounds of chemo, and then we would go back home. During the time at home, he usually had to be brought to the hospital in Pensacola because he would get an infection with a high fever. It was an endless cycle. Our life was not our own. The medical realm is another world.

After my son was diagnosed with cancer, I experienced that I needed God, *big time*. When I started spending time with God, he spoke to me very clearly. So many things had happened. I had lost my husband, my best friend, and my connection to God's love for me. When I started searching and crying out to God, he gently brought me close to him. I remember being led to daily Mass. When I went to Mass, I experienced such peace. At times, it was a little hard, because I cried during the Consecration every time. I didn't want people seeing me crying every week, or for that matter, crying every day. But I felt a closeness to Dav there. Yet as time went on, it was as if Dav disappeared, and it was Jesus, my Savior, who became my rock, the solid foundation to my faith.

CHAPTER 22

DAV'S WORDS OF ENCOURAGEMENT

My faith journey was transformed into a whole new beginning for me. Around this time, I came across a journal Dav had been keeping for the last year, which I did not know about. He had started it in January 1995, from a retreat he went on. He stopped journaling for our three-week summer trip. In August, he started writing again. In September, we started writing to one another—something we learned in Marriage Encounter and practiced at different times of our marriage. We would write to each other on a particular subject and share what we wrote with one another on a date night or before we went to bed, when we were finally alone. This was a great tool for us in keeping communication open. In October, we took a week and wrote about each one of our children, their strengths and their weaknesses. Those are special treasures for me.

That journal was a big part of my transformation and clinging to the cross and not running from it. I would like to share some of the entries from that journal. The words and phrases in parentheses are me sharing my thoughts.

Dav's journaling consisted of him reading from a New American Bible and then meditating on it and writing his thoughts of what it said to him.

January 1, 1995
Psalm 39

Making the most of life. Life is fragile and short. My life is so short. Why do I waste time doing meaningless things? Why do I tell the kids, I don't have time for them?

(I have to make a comment about this sentence. When Danny read that part, he stopped and commented, "Dad always had time for us. What did he mean?" I explained that Dad put higher expectations on himself, and he just wished he spent more time with them.)

What's really important? Put God first. What does that mean? How can I know what's important. This time reflecting and writing? Chris is waiting for me to play pool. Is this more important? How can I know how to spend my time? Time is so precious. When to sharpen the saw? When to work? When to play? I want to spend time with the kids— the boys camping, sailing—is this important. It's not important what we do as long as we spend time together.

(This was the first journal entry I read. I cried and cried. Life is so fragile. That's why I have given my life for these kids—so they would know Christ, and we can all spend all eternity together. This life is fragile and short compared to eternity. What an incredible life to live for. That's the goal, eternity with God.)

January 2, 1995
James 4:13–17

We make plans and have expectations. I should say, if it is the Lord's will. We should not boast about our plans. Humbly say, "If it is the Lord's will." Will I even be around to do this or that? We're planning our vacation, planning the progressive dinner, planning our children's lives. It's okay to have plans and dreams and expectations—but know, only if God wills it. We should pray about our plans and be open to God's will for our lives. Be flexible. If it doesn't turn out the way we expect, accept it as God's will. If I know God's will and do not do it, I am sinning.

(This journal entry, I am sinning if I know God's will and do not do it, kept reminding me to keep seeking God's will and have the courage to do it.)

January 3, 1995
Job 13:1–15

Trust God in times of trial. It's easy to trust in God and appear strong in faith when things are going well. Times of trial, pain, and suffering, it's hard to trust God. Yet that is when we can be drawn closer to God, we can experience his love the most. When Mom died, did I turn to God? I did, but it was still painful. It was hard. It's hard to realize that God uses times of trial, pain, and suffering to make us strong and more like him. It's like to push myself to improve, to accomplish something. Work hard to feel joy of achievement.

January 4, 1995
Acts 2:29–39

Decide to accept Jesus. I have decided to accept Jesus as my Lord and Savior. I have decided to follow him. How do I know his will for my life? His will is for me to stay home on Wednesday nights. I should seek his guidance in everything. Ask for the knowledge of his will. Sometimes I feel empowered I am free to make my own decisions. But I know God loves me, and if I know him, I'll make the right decisions. Bo's funeral today reminded me [to] begin with the end in mind. A lot of friends, good things said, what matters most is what God thought. What does God think of me?

(Dav went out and played basketball with the guys on Wednesday nights, and at the time, I wanted him to stay home. I was being selfish. He needed to do something healthy and active with the guys.)

January 8, 1995
1 John 2:24–3:2

Keep what you first heard in you. Stick to the basic truth that God loves us. The basics are so important in anything; the [basis] of marriage is love for each other. The [basis] of our relationship with God is that he loves us. As I focus on this basic truth, I can love myself and others, knowing that God loves me. Nothing I do can earn me a place in heaven. Without faith and God's love for me, I cannot reach eternal happiness. My actions must reflect my belief. I know Christ will return. What must I change? Accepting his love and forgiveness is the basis [of] faith that will drive my actions.

(I needed to read and reread this entry for it to really sink in. Accepting his love and forgiveness is the basis of faith that will drive my actions.)

January 22, 1995
Ecclesiastes 11

All the good we do, the love we share, [and] the help we give [have] not gone to waste. We may not always see the results or experience a return, but in God's time, it will bear fruit. This is especially true with the kids. We teach them, train them, encourage them, and it never seems to take. But hopefully, when it counts, the kids will make the right decision. The love we give them will bear fruit. Lord, help me to persevere, continue to love, share our faith, teach our children, and have faith.

January 25, 1995
Exodus 33:1–11

Moses spoke to God as a friend speaks to a friend—face to face—in the pillar of cloud. When I speak to God, I don't always realize his presence. My conversations are sometimes one-sided. I do all the talking. I need to listen more. Moses was the chosen one to have an intimate relationship with God. Jesus came so that we can all have that intimate relationship. The Holy Spirit dwells in us so we can converse with God. I must remove distractions to be attentive to

God, to talk, to listen, to offer up my fears, and accept God's peace and love.

(I realized I needed to have a serious committed prayer life.)

February 6, 1995
Psalm 90

Our time on earth is limited. What kind of focus or attitude will we have in our old age? I can get wrapped up in all my problems and projects and forget what's really important. Last week, while Dor was gone, I read the scriptures and took time to pray and experience God's love. It gave me the strength to make it through the week being "calm." Lord help me to focus on what's important and find that prayer time and time to read and meditate on your word—time to read and study and become more like you.

February 10, 1995
1 Thessalonians 4:13–18

Consolation for the grieving. Christians take comfort when loved ones die, knowing that they're in heaven with Jesus. Belief in life after death lessens our blow, our loss. We miss our deceased friends and family, but we can take comfort knowing that they are with God. Life gets tough sometimes, but death could be darker if we don't have the hope of life with God.

(This one was hard to swallow when I was in such pain, but it called me on to go deeper, to believe beyond belief. It helped me start seeing the bigger picture. Eternity with God.)

February 13, 1995
Acts 26:1–23

Responsibility. I am responsible for my own wrongdoings. I cannot blame someone else. Admitting responsibility allows me to ask for forgiveness. Saint Paul persecuted Christians, but Jesus called him to be a leader. Being able to admit his wrong doings, drew others to Christ because of the drastic change. Someone who always does good, does not change, [and] never admits mistakes is hard to believe [and] has low credibility. Lord, help me to admit my mistakes and be able to share them honestly and ask for forgiveness humbly. Help me to let go of past mistakes, accept your forgiveness, and move on to continue to do your work and worship you.

February 16, 1995
John 10:1–15

Jesus is the gate and the good shepherd. I often pray for guidance. But what I need is a guide to lead me every step of the way. Guidance is words telling me what to do and what not to do. But a guide takes me by the hand and leads me, safely and gently, making the decisions. Less effort required on my part, only trust, trust in my guide; confident that he will lead me to safety. Do I trust Jesus to be my guide? Do I put my trust and confidence in him? He is God. If I can't trust him, who can I trust? Lord, I do trust you. There's no need for me to worry. You will protect me and lead me—safely, gently, and confidently.

February 23, 1995
Ephesians 4:1–6

Saint Paul encourages Christians to act as one. United in Christ:

one Spirit, one God, and one Father. We can disagree on minor issues as long as we agree on loving the Lord. Remember what's important. We love and support each other because we see Christ in each other. When I hear the kids arguing over nothing, I just want it to stop. Just treat each other with kindness and respect. Be nice to one another. Lord, I call on you and the power of your love and Your Holy Spirit to unite these children in love. Help Dor and I to express your love for them so they can love each other.

February 26, 1995
Habakkuk 3:17–19

Why me? About our hardships, why me? About our blessings. Sometimes, I think of all the blessings God has given me. I feel guilty and wonder when he will take it away. I don't deserve all the blessings—a wonderful wife, six children, a good job. I secretly look for devastation to come to me, my family. Why do I do that? It's like I don't want to just enjoy it. Maybe that's how Chris feels. He's afraid to just enjoy it. Afraid to count on it. Maybe I'm afraid to count on it. There is so much change taking place now. God's love is the only unchanging thing for us to hold on to.

(I also experienced being afraid of enjoying life. It is like waiting for the other shoe to drop. I have to keep remembering that God's love is unchanging, and I am to trust.)

Ash Wednesday March 1, 1995
1 Corinthians 9:24–27

Athletes train so they can win a perishable prize. We should train spiritually so as to win the imperishable prize. Discipline is very important: to turn away from sin, to put away sinful thoughts. But I cannot do it on my own. I must turn my heart to God as the athlete turns his heart to the prize. I must turn my heart to God out of love for God. I discipline myself to turn away from sin. My ideals, my principles, my values are in God and from God. I chose God's way and not the sinful way.

March 4, 1995
1 Corinthians 13

Love is the essential ingredient. We can have faith, be prayerful [and] spiritual, read scripture, prophesy—all this stuff—but without love, we are nothing. But what is love? Love is caring, caring about someone or yourself, having compassion, being merciful to someone who has hurt you, wanting good to come to others. That is what love is to me. Love is used a lot to describe other things. Love makes you feel good when you give it or receive it. God is Love. When we truly love, we are experiencing God. Love is the attitude or motivation we should have for doing good works. Love allows us to see good in other people, to encourage them and lift them up. Love is a decision.

March 22, 1995
Matthew 5:17–19 Psalm 119:97-104

Heaven and earth will pass away, but the word will last. Wisdom is found through God's word. The written word lasts longer than the spoken word. Books have been written thousands of years ago and can still be read today. I can read and study science and obtain all the worldly knowledge, but true wisdom comes from God's word. The scriptures, inspired by the Holy Spirit, contain truth and knowledge beyond human wisdom. Jesus called us to live a counterculture, the opposite of what the world teaches us. Love my enemy, pray for those who hurt me. This way of life gives us power over the world. When I'm angry or upset or disappointed, I can find peace and wisdom and power through the words of Jesus—the attitude, the vision, his way of life—to live and have eternal life. Help me to turn to your word daily and often, in prayer, to seek your wisdom in your word.

March 27, 1995
Philippians 1:15–26

If you are ready to die, you are ready to live without fear. If I'm faced with death, will I accept it peacefully as going to be with God in heaven? Death is harder on the living—those left behind. Realizing that Jesus is my Lord and Savior should give me a peace about dying. Am I ready to die? My family is not ready for me to die.

(I had to stop there for a while to embrace the pain and sob. No, I was not ready for him to die.)

But I should be ready spiritually—ready to see God. And knowing that I'm ready to die should help me to live without fear, knowing that God loves me, no matter what. Lord, thank you for the weekend, the kids, and the good time we spent together. Help me to spend time with them—special time, one-on-one and together.

(We did do that, and that was a comfort for me. I remember one Lent we chose to take each child out for dinner, an all-you-can-eat kind of place with a great dessert bar, spending special quality time just with that child. To us, Lent was not only about giving up something, which we did do, but it was also about doing something you knew you should be doing that was hard to do. They still talk about that special time with Mom and Dad all to themselves.)

March 28, 1995
John 5:1–16

Jesus heals the man at the pool: take up your mat and walk. He was sick for thirty-eight years. Jesus told him to give up his sins so something worse would not happen to him. What could be worse than being sick for thirty-eight years? If I live in fear, it's worse than being sick. If I get my strength from knowing God loves me, I can live without fear.

(Fear has been one of the biggest obstacles in my life. I thank God for the people who surrounded me and the opportunities of retreats—to be prayed with—at the various times of my life.)

April 17, 1995
Job 14

Despair and hope. Our time on this earth is very limited. A short time in all eternity. If I live in despair, feeling sorry for myself, I'm usually in sin. If I have hope—hope for the future—here on earth and after death, I do so by faith. Believing in the Resurrection, knowing that Jesus died for my sins and atoned for my wrong doings, this hope helps me to do the right things, to love others. Life won't always be a bed of roses; I'll still have my struggles and pain. But in faith, I offer them up to God and believe he will heal me and love me and take care of me.

(This particular journal entry really hit me hard. At the time,

I was still experiencing despair, feeling sorry for myself. I could almost hear my husband saying this to me: "Dor, wake up. You have to have hope," It was so strong and real. I still get choked up when I read this entry. We will always have the struggles and pain of life. I need to recommit daily to do God's will to love and believe in his mercy.)

May 3, 1995
Genesis 5:18–24

Continuing spiritual growth. Do I continually grow in my faith, my spiritual life, my relationship with God? Prayer, scripture reading, reflection, sharing, these are the ways to grow. Life's everyday responsibilities distract me—but should they? Shouldn't I look at them with God's eyes, see them as opportunities to experience God? My goal and vision [are] to embrace everyday life and mesh it with spiritual life, [and] recognizing Satan's attempts to lead me astray, to prayerfully consider each decision, each move, to be led by God in everything, taking opportunities to lift up and encourage people. Help me to make you, Jesus, a part of my everyday life.

(Our life is a journey; I don't have to be perfect today. I just need to work on today. This was one of the last journal entries before our summer trip. He wrote this next one before we started to write to each other. His last entry was two days before his accident.)

August 21, 1995
Matthew 18:10–14

Parable of the lost sheep. If one of a hundred goes astray, the shepherd worries about the one and goes looking for it—and rejoices very much when he finds it. So it is with God; while he loves us all, he rejoices when a stray returns. So it is with me. I worry more about the one child giving me the most trouble and rejoice when he does something to make me proud. The one requires more work that the other five. Lord, help me to rejoice and work for the one stray sheep and be thankful for the ninety-nine.

(I had to have a grateful heart; that is what most of the entries said to me. I had to always look for the good and acknowledge the numerous things to be grateful for. Being grateful makes me happy.)

(This entry was a letter to me. We both read Hebrews 2:1–3 and then wrote what it said to us.)

Hebrews 2:1–3

Dear Dor,

Turn our minds to what has been taught to us. This reminds me of how we learned to dialogue and got away from it. We really do need to dialogue—to focus more on each other. We know we love each other. We get so excited about our growing relationship with God— we want others to grow. But we need to focus on each other, share our thoughts and feelings, and grow more deeply in love with each other, so our children can feel it, see it, and gain security from it. I love you so much, but we get so busy; it scares me that we don't have or take time for each other. All the things that we've experienced together in the past twenty years, the periods of closeness, and the profound movement of God in our life, I feel like I miss it. But yet I know God is still very much a part of us. Preparing for the family

retreat and the upcoming Marriage Encounter weekend makes me
remember all the powerful emotions on all those weekends. I'm so
excited about the Charismatic Conference coming up. I just feel like
praising God and thanking him for all that has happened to us and
is still happening to us.

    I lov you, Dav

I treasure those letters from him, and from time to time I will reread them. The wide variety of topics we covered those last five months was amazing. One can get a glimpse of the profound words that were left for me to cling to so as to have hope for the future. I couldn't give up.

CHAPTER 23

ABANDONMENT AND HEALING

As my desire for God grew, I experienced a stumbling block to God the Father. I had a good relationship with Jesus and the Holy Spirit, but with God the Father something was not right. I had a friend who was a religious, Brother Stephen, with whom I was sharing this part of my spiritual block. We had known him for a few years, and he knew about my parents and my relationship with my father. He gently asked, "Have you ever considered reconciling with your father?"

You would have thought he had said the most horrible thing to me. I responded with throwing every pillow on my couch (there were many) across the room at him and yelling, "Dav would never have abandoned these children, as hard as it has been. My father left me." I said other things too, but you get the gist.

What surfaced was how abandoned I felt by my father and that I had felt no real love from him. I was twenty-one and had been married for three years when my parents started divorcing. It was amazing how, as an adult, I still felt that abandonment and rejection.

As I reflected on my emotional upheaval that day, I realized that I saw God the Father through my father and how I perceived his love for me. It was a greatly distorted image of God the Father, which was not the truth. My perception of my father was, if he did something for you, you owed him, big time. I experienced his love for me as manipulative, and God is not manipulative. It became clearer to me that God the Father sent his Son to suffer and die for us so that we might be saved, to live in eternity with him forever. That is love that we, as humans, really cannot fully grasp. But my husband had showed me a tiny glimpse of unconditional love. I knew God's love was much more than that. Dav's journal opened a door to my soul and deeper desire for God.

Brother Stephen left rather quietly and returned a few days later. I was in the backyard, cleaning the pool, as he came around the corner of the house. He yelled, "Is it safe to come over?"

I responded, "Yeeaah, no pillows this time."

As we talked, he recommended I write a letter to my father but instructed me to pray before I began. He suggested that I not write about blame and stay away from saying "you" but use "I" instead. When he left, he added, "You don't really have to mail it."

Not long after Danny's diagnosis, we were in Gainesville, and I had more time alone. It was time to write the letter to my father. I can vividly remember that evening. I was sitting on the twin bed in Wayne's extra room. Danny and Wayne were chatting in the living room and watching a sports event. I had the Bible next to me and a notebook. I asked the Holy Spirit to help me and guide me. I wanted to not blame or speak negatively in this letter. I had many hurts about my father that I really had not dealt with yet. I opened to scripture for guidance a few times and then began to write the letter. That opened the door to my relationship with my earthly father. A wall was removed, and I was able to experience God the Father. It was like stepping out of the boat into an unknown and trusting God would be there.

I did mail the letter, and I received a letter not long after from my father. Communication was opened. I still had apprehensions about my father controlling me, in the sense that I owed him. I made a plan to visit him when I was in Biloxi by myself. I was not ready to let the kids meet him. Our visit went well. I brought pictures of the six kids. I had fears he would not accept the biracial girls, and I was not going to let them experience any rejection from him. My fears disappeared. He thought our family was beautiful. He said he was proud of what Dav and I had done. The icing on the cake was when I sent him a card for his birthday with money in it. I received a letter back with the money and a note for me to spend it on the children. That act of his took away the feelings of me owing my father anything. It was only love he wanted.

As I reflect on those crosses, those six short weeks after Dav died, I see a pattern being opened up. I needed to be healed of my relationship with my earthly father to be able to have faith in God the Father. I needed to be freed from the fear of not going outside in the back where Dav had fallen. I needed to experience a physical healing of my breathing attacks to know, without a doubt, that God was going to take care of me. When I look at my crosses as teaching me and helping me to be the person God wants me to be, they are sweet. Thanking God is the key to all of this for me. The lives of the saints are the maps we need to help us on the journey on earth to reach the destination of eternity in heaven with God.

CHAPTER 24

ANGELS UNAWARE

I believe and trust in God's plan for my life. The stories that follow are of the mercy and care God has provided for me. I hope they inspire you to seek God first in all things.

My parish family and friends in Pensacola took such good care of us. For six months or more after Dav's death they brought us meals—not every day, but enough to help with planning. People would randomly drop off paper products. I had one woman come and clean my house on a couple of occasions. God just kept bringing people in our life who were helping. Our home felt like it had a revolving door, which I experienced as a blessing. It was a great witness of God's love. Our family from Biloxi was also an incredible support, coming weekend after weekend. We were loved tangibly, as Christ loves us through our family and friends.

As the months went by, it became harder on Danny to take

the six-hour drive to Gainesville. Brother Stephen knew a man, Arthur, who was retired and had a small plane. He told him our story, and Arthur flew us many times, for free. God be praised—another gift.

Father Mike knew a woman from his past parish. Right before he went over to tell her about our family, she was watching EWTN and she had just asked God in her heart, *What do you want me to do?* Father Mike knocked on her door, told her our story, and asked if she could come and help with the kids. I will always think of her as my special angel. Loretta was amazing: very structured and organized, and she loved to clean. Did I forget to mention that she was in her seventies? She had been in the army, and her husband had died. She had two sons. One had died of cancer in his twenties, and her other son lived in California with his wife. She had a great sense of humor too. She told you what was on her mind, with blunt honesty and great love. I always smile when I think of her. When she was at my house, she followed my rules, but when we went to visit her at her house, we followed her rules. She would offer the kids a soda and a snack and with her military voice say, "Don't look at your mother; what soda do you want?" We never had soda in our house except for really special occasions. I cannot say enough what a gift she was to our family. The children needed structure while I was away, and Loretta was that for them.

During that first summer, two men showed up at my house. One was the son of a friend from church. He had a construction business, and, as a gift, he wanted to finish what Dav had been working on. I became overwhelmed; I ran to my room, crying. When I came back down, they were still there—they needed me to tell them what I wanted done. I accepted their help. What an act of kindness and generosity. They finished the outside and then finished the laundry and art room. Praise God.

CHAPTER 25

HOMESCHOOL BONDING

The kids had finished school, and it was summer. The three younger ones could not get out of their slump and focus on their school work. They would probably need to stay back the next year. I had experienced that people felt sorry for them, and the kids were not held accountable for much. They had acquired bad habits that needed to be addressed. The kids had redefined procrastinating to the extreme.

My friend Toni told me she was going to homeschool her five children in the coming school year. I had brought the subject up to her a year or so before, but now I thought, *Not now*. I knew I had to seriously pray about this. I did, and I came to the conclusion that I needed to pull the reins in on the family. Plans for homeschooling began.

Homeschooling children who had experienced the outside

world and a school atmosphere was challenging. I did not let much slip by me though. At times, I wished I did not notice so much, but my conscience would not let things go. I was told I could do twenty things at once. I realize the gifts we have are wonderful, but they can also be a burden. Staying on top of everything had to be all God.

Ever since we had adopted the last three children, family life was harder. They immediately went off to school or preschool, and there was homework and baths and dinner and chores. Life was going too fast—there had been no time to bond as a family, and summers were too short.

It was even more difficult with Danny being sick; we all needed to pull together. It may have been easier to let them be in school all day and only have to care for them the short few hours before bedtime, but there was so much to teach. I knew I needed to be consistent and strong for them to experience unconditional love. The bottom line was I knew it was God's will to homeschool now. With them being homeschooled our schedule was flexible, we could go to Biloxi for a visit anytime that worked for Danny. There was some good benefits for the family.

My relationship with my husband was such that he had heard all my frustrations, and I was beginning to miss Dav terribly. He had been tangible, and I wanted tangible. This was an area where I needed to grow—God needed to be my all. Each time I ran to God for help, which seemed like daily if not hourly, when I sat and listened, I just kept hearing, "Love them."

Most of the time, my response was, "I can't. You have to love them through me; you have to do it." It was too hard. I wanted a road map to tell me what "love them" meant.

My crying eventually stopped for Dav, yet my tears and crying out to God for these children was ever so intense. My heart ached for them. At times I felt I was in a war zone with them against me and the fight was intense. I was so weary, yet every time I went to God, he renewed me. I would go to scripture and ask for advice and hear God's word to me about my situation almost every time. The times when I wanted to give up the fight, the scripture would be "children obey your parents." I had no idea that there were so many different places in the Bible that referred to obedience to parents. This encouraged me, and I knew I had to keep going. Other times, when we went to daily Mass, the priest would give a three-liner homily, and it would speak to the children so clearly that they would ask, "Did you talk to Father about that?" No, I had not, although frequently the topic was the same lecture I had given to them that morning in the car on the way to church. Those were the times I experienced God working so powerfully in my life.

Now that Autumn is older, she has said that what she remembers the most was that I never gave up on her. I would be in her face day after day, correcting but also repeating over and over, "You are a daughter of God." That was the bottom line, and she needed to act like it. We had started training our children to answer the question "Who are you?" with "I am a son [or daughter] of God." So each night, when we did our goodnight ritual, we asked that question. Sometimes, in the heat of a discussion, I would remind them of who they were and ask if they were acting like a daughter or son of God. This sometimes diffused the argument.

I had the curriculum set for each child, and each child knew what assignments needed to be completed each day. The friends who helped out while I was away with Danny could follow my curriculum. I wanted to give up many times, but was reminded this is God's will not mine.

We finished the school year, thank God. I believe that we all learned valuable lessons—perseverance for one, which can help anyone get through life. It was an incredible challenge to say the least. I could see good coming from it, which helped me keep going.

CHAPTER 26

MY PRAYER TIME

God was about, doing many things in my life. I had a committed prayer time each day: morning, early evening, and bedtime with the *Liturgy of the Hours*. This book is used mostly by the religious, but it has started to become popular with the lay people. It is incredible to think that thousands of people are saying those prayers, and we are all being united together. It just helped me to know I was not alone. I was reminded of the spaghetti story and the child with the "my playtime" scenario—how our children can be a reflection of ourselves if we look close enough and how they can teach us. I came to the conclusions that these children were gifts, and they were helping me get to heaven. That was my life's goal now.

My Morning Prayer time was easy; I could get up earlier than anyone else, which was something I did not do much before my husband died. I had thought I required ten or more hours of rest most times. I laugh at myself now. The bedtime was also easy. The early evening slot I chose to commit to was ten to fifteen minutes between five and seven o'clock. Each day may have been at a slightly different time, but I felt I had to give myself a timeframe to reach for. I wonder now as I look back over the years what was I thinking? I had six small, demanding children, and I was trying to do something during the worst time of the day. But that was where I received my strength and where God taught me valuable lessons.

Every time I prayed during that early evening time. I would end up coming out of my room fussing about how they should be doing this or that—not the arguing that was going on. One time, as I tried to go back to my prayer time after I had done a lot of correcting—and not peacefully I might add—I gently heard God in my heart, *Is that how you think I would want you to handle that?*

In my head, I said, *What would you want me to do?*

I heard, *Take care of them.*

And not have prayer time? That didn't make sense to me. The next day, I thought I had them all doing something that would keep them occupied for ten or fifteen minutes. I went to my room, but as soon as I knelt down and made the sign of the cross, I heard screaming.

I said, "Okay, Lord, caring for them is my prayer time," and I blessed myself again. I got up and calmly disbursed the fighting, redirected them, and began finishing up for dinner.

The next day, I went to have prayer time in the early evening again. I am very persistent. God blessed me: no disruptions. I wondered what it meant. I felt God say, *It's about obedience.* I needed to be obedient in the small ways, just as I expected the children to be obedient. My thinking that prayer time was more important than being obedient to God was wrong. It was about listening to God and acting on it. I prayed during that time of day for about ten years. In the beginning, my attitude during that time was "This is my prayer time, do not disturb it," which I came to understand was not correct. Even if they came to my door needing me to answer a question, I was not happy.

On one occasion, after this lesson from God, Josh, who was three at the time, came to my door and was putting his fingers under the door yelling excitedly about something he wanted me to come see. When I opened the door, my past response might have been a scolding. This time, I knelt down and looked at him and asked in a gentle voice, "What does it mean when Mommy's door is closed?"

He excitedly said, "Oh, I forgot," and as he ran off, he added, "I'll show you later." Which he did.

I wasn't out of peace anymore. God was doing amazing things.

CHAPTER 27

DANNY'S TWO YEARS

That first year of treatment was intense—nothing I had ever experienced. Danny was a piece of work. You had to laugh at him. He always said what was on his mind, and he had much to say in the beginning of his illness. He hated needles. It was such an ordeal each time he was stuck, which was often. He eventually trained himself to act more tolerant so that everyone else did not hear his objections. He and I started a joke between us; when something seemed hard for me, he would say, "Offer it up, Mom," and I would say it back to him when he was dealing with something that was hard for him. It helped us to keep giving it back to God. I saw it as embracing the cross and we received so much grace from God to keep going.

Once, the homebound teacher said to me, "He is such a good kid, every time I go by his room to check up on him he is always smiling, and when I ask him if he needs anything he usually responds with 'I'm okay.'" But in reality, he was always in pain and a bit lonely. This was a teenager who did not have a TV or video games in his room. He had Legos and books or regular board games. I never was one to let the children sit in front of the TV or watch videos when they did not feel well.

It was a long Lent that year. I had decided to give up chocolate. Chocolate is my favorite and that is an understatement. It seemed that the hospital would have the most incredible chocolate desserts on the days I decided to not eat chocolate. I felt very strongly that this sacrifice was important. I experienced Christ's passion so real in my life that year. There was a peace and joy in that sacrifice of not eating chocolate that I had never experienced before.

By the end of the school year, I had lost almost fifty pounds. Now everyone was on my case to eat. I had a hard time. I felt like I was eating, just maybe not a lot. I had gotten in the habit of not eating sweets, mostly wanting to offer it as a sacrifice for the kids. I could fit in my wedding dress again, twenty years later. I had weighed ninety-five pounds when I got married. It took almost a year to return to a more normal weight.

In July, Danny had surgery to remove part of his lung. He had six months of treatment. He started losing his hair—literally chunks of it would fall out. He had huge bald spots all over his head. He finally decided to shave it all off. He had no eyelashes, no eyebrows, no hair. He took it all in stride. He also lost weight, and he had been thin to begin with. My twelve-year-old was growing up fast. We were told he was cancer free around February of 1997. It had been a long year for everyone.

In Gainesville, Florida, I met a few people at daily Mass who played a wonderful part in taking care of Danny and me. One couple had us stay at their home when we could not get a room at the McDonald house. Another woman I met at daily Mass let me stay for a few days in their maid's quarters. Another time, Danny and I stayed in their home while they were away. What trust in God for them; we were really total strangers. It was a time when Danny needed to not be around anyone who was sick. It is amazing to look back and see the incredible things God did during that time in Gainesville.

I had a social worker with hospice tell me once, "I see a hurricane whirling all around you, and you are steady as a rock." I have never forgotten that image, and I can see it more clearly now that I am not in the midst of that storm. When I have other storms happening around me, I reflect and remember, *God is in this one too.* Once we had to wait for our appointment for over four hours. We saw the Dr. probably a total of 10 minutes. I could not believe how peaceful I was; even Danny had peace. This had to be of God.

Make a Wish sends the family on a vacation. At first, we were just going to Disney World. In one of our conversations, I mentioned how Danny wanted to catch a marlin in Hawaii. They took that one comment and said, "Okay, you're going to Hawaii." I did not want that extravagant of a trip. It was taken out of my hands, and off we went to Hawaii. He got his wish; out of all the boats in the marina that went out that day, they were the only ones who caught a marlin. It weighed 105 pounds.

Danny also wanted to wind surf, which was extremely hard for him. He was weak and thin, but he got up once and that was enough for him. He loved snorkeling amid the reefs and seeing all the different fish; he loved fish. The whole trip was a wonderful memory for the entire family. A friend, Sue, and her daughter Carrie got to go with us. I felt I needed a few extra adult hands.

In the summer of 1997, Danny's cancer returned. We were told about a procedure called, bone-marrow transplant. It sounded a little risky to me. They would kill everything in his body and then at the right moment give him back his bone marrow to start building up again. This procedure would take six to eight weeks. To leave the other children for that long would be very hard for me. We decided to go for it—what else were we to do. The children would go to Biloxi and be with family that summer.

The process started August 28, 1997. Right before Danny was to go into the hospital for the bone marrow, we went to church in Gainesville for daily Mass. The priest did the intercessory prayer and asked if anyone wanted to add something. A few others did, and I had a sense to pray for Danny's bone-marrow transplant, but I couldn't say it. The priest said a few more intentions and asked again, "Does anyone have an intention?" Again, I couldn't speak up. The priest continued, and for the third time, he asked if anyone else had an intention.

I blurted out, "My son Danny's bone-marrow transplant." I had never heard this priest ask for intentions this way and for so many times. God had wanted me to make this intention known. We received the Eucharist, and afterward, the priest came up to Danny and asked if he would like to be anointed and prayed with. Danny said yes. The priest got a chair and put it at the front of the altar facing the people, and a man brought the oils. The priest invited anyone to come and lay hands on Danny. It was an awesome experience. I know we both received extraordinary graces for the next six to eight weeks.

Day after day, the treatment was bombarding his body with drugs to kill everything. He had become thin and frail looking, and this made it even worse. When I look at the pictures now, I can't believe how bad he looked. But I was in the midst of the forest and did not see much beyond the moment I was in. I played very soothing Christian music around the clock in his room. The nurses loved coming in; they would comment how peaceful it was to come in his room. There was not much to do but just be. It was a wonderful opportunity to read and pray. I read lives of the saints, prayed the rosary, and said the divine mercy prayer and read the bible. It was a gift to have so much time with God. I knew people were praying for us and sacrificing for us. I felt an incredible peace. I lived at the Ronald McDonald house during those weeks, just a place to lay my head. For almost twelve days Danny did not eat, and for almost seven days he did not drink. He started out taking a few pieces of ice one day, and I wrote excitedly on a calendar I kept, in big letters, "YEAH!! Ate a few pieces of ice." Each day, I would come back to my room and put a big X over that day with a sigh of relief. We were closer to the end. The symptoms from the drugs on his body were a high fever for days and horrible mouth sores, which went all the way down the throat and into the stomach. At one point, they drugged him so he would stay asleep the whole day. His body needed the rest. It was extremely difficult to see him in such pain. It was an incredible time of loneliness, yet God kept placing people in my life at the right moments.

Another summer ended, and things were good. Danny took a while to recoup. His hair grew back full and wavy; it had been straight and thin before. His skin was like a baby's. His energy level was the last to return to a somewhat normal pace.

Father Mike kept mentioning that someone he knew wanted to send Danny to Lourdes, France, where Mary had appeared. It was a place known for healings. I had said no previously, but Father Mike kept mentioning it, and I finally agreed. Danny was going in November, and he would be there for his fourteenth birthday. It was an incredible experience for him. Father Mike took him, and they stayed with people Father Mike knew. Danny was able to go to the baths in Lourdes on two occasions. He told me that he received a deep peace and an internal healing about his life on that trip. I have to say, he was different when he returned.

We had an appointment with the doctors' right after Christmas of 1997, and they told us the cancer was back. It was in his lungs. They proceeded to tell us about our next options. They left the room for a few minutes, and I remember Danny looking at me very seriously, and he said, "I don't want any more treatments. I think we are messing with God's plan."

That was a hard pill to swallow. I felt the same but in a sad sort of way. I had a great relationship with Danny. At one point, Dav had said in one of our dialogues that he envied the relationship Danny and I had. Twice I had felt that Danny should have died: on the pool ladder at his grandparents and when he followed his dad onto the beach across a four-lane highway. Now, watching him suffer was extremely painful. Yet I felt I had to be strong for everyone else. So I continued and walked alone, crying out to God, and I experienced peace.

There are no words to express what the last three months were like. The cancer spread from his lungs to his brain. Toward the end, his eyesight diminished, and he barely ate anything.

There were many friends who came and spent the night in the spare room with a monitor to hear Danny because I needed a break. Danny needed meds throughout the night. Some friends would even stay in his room and sleep in a recliner. My friends were incredible. The family in Biloxi came on the weekends and helped. Another friend made a chart of all the meds and the times, so everyone knew what Danny had taken last. We had to initial the chart each time we gave him something. He was taking so many different meds and at so many different times, it was very confusing. With so many people coming and helping with his meds the chart was such a blessing.

It was Thursday, March 19, 1998. Dav had died only two years earlier-on January 19. Hospice had stayed overnight the night before for the first time. I went in to see what Danny wanted for breakfast. He had not been eating much for days. He asked for French toast, scrambled eggs, and bacon. I tried to change his mind. I'm thinking how much time that would take to prepare and he is not eating enough for a bird. I had some great muffins, waffles but nothing doing, that was what he wanted. So I made it all and sent one of the kids up with it.

I was in the forest and couldn't see the trees. I went in to check on him a little later. I saw that he had almost eaten all of it, which was surprising. I started talking to him, and he seemed to not be responding very well. The hospice nurse checked him and told me to call the family; it would be soon. His body was shutting down, and he had fallen into a comma state.

We called the family. Some came within a couple of hours: my husband's brother Paul (Danny's godfather), his wife Karen, my niece Jorrie, and my sister Lila (Danny's godmother). We prayed the rosary throughout the day many times. We did a novena to Saint Joseph because it was the feast of Saint Joseph. Every half hour we would stop everything and say the novena prayer which we did nine times that day in his room. I was begging God to not let him die on the nineteenth, as I would be so fearful of that date. The day dragged on. Father Mike came, and Diane, homebound teacher, was there that day too. Many other friends came by. I had one friend tell me later that Danny's room was so peaceful and filled with grace so thick that she did not want to leave. I have to agree, it was an incredible experience—a holy death.

Around three in the afternoon (the divine mercy hour) Danny

awoke and asked, "What are ya'll doing." He acted like nothing had happened.

His uncle Paul responded, "Where having a party."

I decided to have each child spend a few minutes alone with him. Father Mike offered him the Eucharist, and he said, "Yes."

When Chris and Josh were in there, his last words to them were, "Be good." Then he drifted off into the coma state again.

The day went into evening. My friend Brother Stephen, the friend I had thrown all the pillows at, had come into town and was giving a retreat for men in the diocese, which started the next evening. Before he left he said, "You call me if you need anything, no matter what time it is."

It was getting late. Father Mike left by eleven o'clock, and everyone in the house was settling in for the night. The children all went to friends' homes for the night—except for Danah. The hospice nurse and Diane stayed.

I was finally alone with Danny. I sat Indian style at the end of his bed. I had the Bible and was reading scripture aloud to him. At one point, I told him, "I am going to be alright, God is going to take care of me. You can go see God." I felt I needed to help him let go.

As I sat there, it was around midnight, and I started to get the idea to call Brother Stephen. My stubbornness kept me from calling; I felt I shouldn't bother him. But after about a half hour, I finally did call; he was only a few blocks away. Dav's brother Paul, Brother Stephen, and I sat around Danny's bed, reminiscing about both Dav and Danny and laughing. Diane came up behind me and placed her hand on my back and said, "He's going home; you need to pray."

I was taken aback, but Brother Stephen placed his hands on Danny and started praying, and I followed his lead. Paul jumped up and got everyone else in the house. As they are coming in, Danny took his last breath.

There are really no words to explain it. It was an incredible peaceful moment. Even though, as I write this, I am filled with tears and a welling sensation of emotions, the peace was incredible. It was not anything like Dav's sudden death. I told the nurse to take the tubes out of him; I didn't want them in there anymore. Danny had hated all that stuff. I wanted it gone. She did.

Then I told everyone, "I'm really sorry to do this again to ya'll, but I need to say the rosary again right now." I needed Mary's comfort as a mother. We must have said six or more rosaries that day. I knelt on the floor, and we prayed.

Afterward, my sister and I went downstairs, and we just sat on the couch in silence. It was a different numbness compared to Dav's death. We waited till after all the legalities were done with hospice. Then the funeral home came and picked Danny up. I felt heaven was crying with us—a light mist was falling, and I experienced a great comfort. Then I went to my bed and cried till I fell asleep, exhausted. It was over, and, thank God, it was on the twentieth and not the nineteenth.

Now I am in a different place, and I think that dying on the feast of Saint Joseph would have been a wonderful thing. Yet the day itself was a gift, and God gave Danny back to us for a brief time at the three o'clock hour of mercy. I can only say, "Praise be to God." It was such a special gift to care for him those last months. I know I was given special graces from God, because it was such a joy for me even in the tiredness.

I really did not realize the loss for the children until later. They had lost their dad and six weeks later Danny was diagnosed with cancer. I was gone a lot for the next two years with him. There were so many things changing constantly in our lives—everything except God. All I could do was trust in him and in his love for us. I was being asked to walk on water.

Before Danny died, especially during those last few months, I would massage his back at night before I went to bed. He was not getting out of bed much, and his body was in constant pain. Those were precious times of sharing. We never saw eye to eye about the TV or computer games or music. But he had become so respectful and obedient to anything I said that there was never an issue. So I had asked him if he would send me a sign after he died if I was right about TV. He had asked me what I wanted, and I responded, "A white rose." And then I asked him, if he was right what would he send? He replied, "An orange rose."

He and Father Mike had planned his wake and funeral mass. What he would wear, the color theme, the scriptures. He had become an avid Gator fan, and their colors were orange and blue. He had said he would send me an orange rose—uh huh.

That evening at the wake, my sister suggested we go look at the flowers. Danny had picked an orange Bird of Paradise for the casket, and he wore a Gator bow tie. The only roses in the place were in an arrangement on a four-foot vine cross—there were white roses going down the middle.

When I saw those roses, that conversation with Danny about TV came back to my memory. It filled me with great confidence to keep going. I had been second-guessing myself at that time. This was truly God's plan. There should always be caution with anything that takes more precedence over our relationship with God. Everything in our life is about balance. That was my whole issue with TV, music, and video games: balance.

Chapter 28

Remembrance Stories

Some of my prize possessions were the family albums we had of our memory trips and holidays. I had made captions and cute sayings for many of the pictures. One of the times I was away with Danny, Chris, who was eleven at the time, decided to make his own album. He used the family albums to try to create his own. Later, I realized that he had taken our albums apart, and he never really finished his. There was a knot in my stomach and a lump in my throat; I just wanted to scream. I decided to not say anything to him. I just threw the pictures and the rest of the albums in a box.

I realized later that Chris was trying to hold on to the family. A family he had known for only four years of his life, and a dad who had spent time with him—a father he loved and felt security with. So much turmoil in his short life.

Rarely did I look at the pictures in that box; I felt as if that was how my life was, a big mess. I didn't want to be reminded of it. On occasion, the children would pull the box out and sit and reminisce. I, on the other hand, could not do it. I believed I had had everything in order—vacations with captions, celebrations, and milestones of everyone's lives. All of that was lost, and my life felt lost.

I held that inside until the winter of 2007. With the prodding of Autumn, then twenty-one, I bought albums and, making the dining room table my office, I started separating the pictures into years and then into seasons. It took over three weeks and seven albums, but the accomplishment and healing I experienced was unbelievable.

For years after Dav died, I would put pictures of our family out in the living room, but it seemed I would put them away after a short time. It was too painful to look at. I wanted to be a family again. I did not feel we were a family. Yet in God's plan we were. After putting the albums back together, something changed. When I put the pictures out again, I had no desire to put them away. A healing had taken place, and now I can say I am grateful for what I was given; I am not dwelling on what I don't have. Praise be to God.

That first year after Dav died, I began to notice the children going into their rooms and just listening to their boom boxes, their stereos. Each child had one, and I started to see that they were using it to escape from life. I made a decision to remove all of them and only have a family-based one in the living room. I took all their CDs away, but I realized beforehand that I needed to replace them with other music. You would have thought World War III had begun.

All five children went crazy. Danny, my sick child, was screaming how Dad gave the boom box to him. That was one of the hardest things I ever had to do, because I knew they were hanging onto anything that had to do with their dad. When I heard Danny's statement, I yelled back, "What makes you think he is not praying to get me to do this? He knows now!" That stopped him in his tracks. It was a very difficult change. I did see the fruit of this in Danny's last days.

This particular story I'm going to share made me see something in a whole new light.

It was a time when Danny was cancer free. I had called Danny down to come and bring Josh, who was two and a half, outside to play. Danny came out of the play room and asked, "Can Chris bring Josh out?" Danny had been in the middle of building "this cool Lego thing."

I responded, "No, I want you to do it."

He came down a couple of steps and was pleading again not to have to bring Josh out.

I went up the steps and met him. I was standing right in front of him with my face in his face. I said, "Have you not figured anything out? What else has to happen to this family? When are you going to get it? Do you see how selfish you are being? Dad played with you. Josh won't ever have that. Wake up."

Then there was silence, and we just looked at each other.

He responded, "Yes, ma'am," and he went and got Josh and brought him outside. I was in the kitchen, being busy, but I checked every once in a while to see if Danny was really interacting with him or if he was sitting on the deck and telling Josh to go play. Danny had gotten the T-ball and bat and ball and was very much interacting with Josh.

After that, I started noticing that every time I asked Danny to do something, he would put a fake smile on his face and say, "Yes ma'am," and he'd go and do it. At first, it was weird, but he kept doing it. One night, at bedtime, as I was going in each child's room to give them their blessing, I decided to ask Danny about it.

"What's with the fake smile and the 'yes ma'am' all about anytime I ask you to do something for me," I asked.

Remember, he was twelve.

He took a deep breath and said, "Well, Mom, I got to thinking. I might die, and I want to go to heaven. And to go to heaven, I need to be obedient."

I felt like I was punched in the stomach. My twelve-year-old son just taught me the most important lesson in life. He got it and was really living it. And he might die too, which became more real to me right then.

I went to my room, got on my knees, and cried, and then I told God I wanted to go to heaven. I wanted to be obedient. I asked him, "Please, help me."

One Lent, after Danny had died, I was meditating on the Stations of the Cross, and one was about Mary seeing her son in such pain; it helped me unite my suffering to hers. I could really relate to her as a mom, watching her child in pain. I think it was the first time I experienced the agonizing in my heart for the times I watched him suffer. Tears welled up inside me. I was able to embrace the cross, and I experienced a sweetness.

Once, on a retreat, I had heard a saying about the three Cs—cry, commit, and continue. Those three words have helped me to know that it is okay to cry. I am human, and humans were made to have feelings and emotions. After Dav died, I cried so much it was scary. For a while, I almost made myself not cry; it was just too painful. After a good cry I am reminded to recommit and continue on this journey.

In the Liturgy of the Hours, the Saturday night prayers, the scripture was from Deuteronomy, and it said, "Hear, O Israel!

The Lord is our God, the Lord alone! Therefore, you shall love the Lord, your God, with all your heart, and with all your soul, and with all your strength. Take to heart these words, which I enjoin on you today. Drill them into your children. Speak of them at home and abroad, whether you are busy or at rest." When I read that, I decided I needed to tell the children; it was important. For months, when I prayed, I asked the Holy Spirit to remind me to do this. But week after week, I would not remember. It got to be an internal pain for me because each Saturday night when I read it, I had not remembered during the week to mention it to the kids. It was a frustration I did not like. I continued though—praying to the Holy Spirit to remind me. I desired so much for the children to know this.

This next story finishes my Saturday night prayer. Our pastor was a great source of support for our family. Father Mike was going to check out the place where the diocese youth groups were going to have a conference. Danny needed an outing. The theme of the conference was Your Lesson in Life. A few months later, Father Mike showed up with a video that someone had put together for him about Danny. At that point, Danny was not leaving his room, and I finally had allowed him a small TV so he could watch movies. I popped the video in, and it started out with beautiful music choreographed to different pictures and a video of Danny. It ended with Danny being interviewed at the conference center that time he went with Father Mike. Danny quoted a scripture and proceeded to say that his lesson in life was: "To love the Lord, your God, with all your heart, mind, and soul ..."

It blew me away. As I sat on the floor, I cried tears of joy, and I got goose bumps all over. I had been begging God to help me to tell my children this at every Saturday night prayer for months, and here all I did was persevere in prayer about it. God answers prayer in his time and in his way, which is always the best way. Sometimes God wants us to repeat over and over truths to our children, and at other times, he just wants us to persevere in prayer for them. Each child is different, and each child's needs are unique.

Not long after Danny died, I became stir crazy and needed something to keep me busy. I was busy with the other five children, but compared to the pace I had been living for those last two years, it was not enough.

I decided to paint my kitchen. In considering the color, I felt as though I needed to do something extreme, out of the box. I chose a Pepto-Bismol pink. The countertops were blue. I am not sure what I was thinking—boy/girl balance? I suppose I could analyze that thinking as wanting balance in my life. Even though, I have to laugh at myself now. It did keep me busy for quite some time. The end result was accomplished. I was very busy.

CHAPTER 29

GOD'S BLESSINGS

For four years after Dav died, I was able to go away almost every six or eight weeks on some sort of retreat. I marvel as I look back on that time, and Danny being sick, yet God literally opened the door for everything. I know that's part of where I received the grace to continue. Dav and I had believed that if the two of us took time for one another on a regular basis, the children would benefit. We were more united and renewed physically and spiritually.

Before Dav died, I was involved with a women's retreat for our diocese. This was one of the things that kept me going. A few other women and I had planned the retreat for that next year. It was a great outlet for me. Father Mike had me making banners for the youth conference. I was also busy with a family retreat, which Dav and I had started a few years before. It was hard, but it was good to be part of something. God was about many things in my life.

A woman I knew in New Jersey from the People of Hope would call on occasion and just touch base, encouraging me and praying with me over the phone. It was much needed. I would experience a peace and courage to keep going from that prayer. She mentioned the community was having Camp Hope for children in August and told me the dates. It stayed on my mind, and I felt we were supposed to go. Josh stayed in Pensacola those two and a half weeks, and I brought the rest of the kids to camp. It was an incredible experience. Danny had a cancer-free window that first summer. I worked in the kitchen the first week, which was very hard work and long hours, yet I felt reenergized spiritually. The second week I was able to go on a silent retreat which was a blessing for me.

The camp was a mixture of fun activities and Mass, adoration, and prayer time. Adoration is an act of worship and devotion to Jesus Christ, made through prayers offered before a consecrated host. The boys and girls had prayer time separately, and then they would get together for adoration.

When the boys were coming into the room for adoration, Danny came and found me and whispered, "Mom, Mom, you won't believe what happened." I did not want him to talk; this was supposed to be a silent time. But I could tell he was very excited. He proceeded to say that the boys had prayed over him, and he felt healed (a weight lifted) about Dad and the accident. He had been blaming himself, believing that he should have been able to help his dad. I could tell he had a joy about him, something was lifted. The rest of the time before the Lord was wonderful. Danny had experienced God's love and mercy. I knew then that Danny would draw his strength from God, and he would be alright spiritually.

During my conversations with my friend from New Jersey, she

mentioned a women's retreat. I flew back down for that retreat in the fall. God just kept loving me in unbelievable ways. The kids went to camp in New Jersey the next few summers, and I was able to go on retreat a few times in the fall.

CHAPTER 30

ROSES

It was October of 1999, and our family was doing a novena for All Saints' Day. A recitation of prayers and devotions for a special purpose during nine consecutive days. I told the children to decide on their own saint to ask for what they wanted, but we as a family would say the novena (the prayers) each day together. On All Saints' Day, which was November 1, we went to the cemetery to change out the flowers and say a prayer for Dav and Danny.

Later that day, Autumn approached me and said she thought her novena was answered—what should she do?

I responded that God usually just takes care of it.

She said she thought I needed to know.

I was reluctant, but I finally agreed. She proceeded to tell me that she had prayed to Saint Sebastian for a red rose if she was to go to Koinonia Academy in New Jersey. When we were at the cemetery, she had seen something on the ground. When she approached it she saw that is was a miniature red rose. As she looked up the name on the headstone was Sebastian.

She said, "Mom, don't you think my prayer was answered?"

My response was, "I'm the head of this household; God has to speak to me."

She replied, "So you'll pray about it?"

I half responded, "I'll pray about praying about it."

This was not the first time she had brought up moving to New Jersey and going to their school. We had been to their camp for the last three years, and she had cried each time we left. But you have to remember, the children always had a hard time moving to the next moment.

Later that day, I happened to go to my room, and I saw a novena to Saint Therese of the Little Flower on my bed. I had prayed many novenas to Saint Therese, and she had given me a specific color rose I had asked for on many occasions. But I couldn't figure out why it was on my bed now. I put it on my prayer table and went about my day. That night, I said my night prayers and went to bed. But I could not sleep; I kept hearing, "Get up and start the novena."

I had a conversation in my head for almost an hour. *God, you can't really want me to leave here. It is too expensive to live in New Jersey. It is too cold. I will miss the beach. No, I can't; this can't be what you want.*

But then I reluctantly threw off my covers and went over to my prayer corner and knelt. I remember saying, matter-of-factly, *Okay, Lord, if you want me to move to New Jersey, I want a pink rose, if not, I want a yellow one.*

I began the novena. Ten days later, I went to see my spiritual director at his parish; they were having adoration that day. I was early for my appointment and decided to visit Jesus. I began to pour my heart out for direction and help. As I left, I saw the statue of Mary and asked her to help me as a mom—this is way too hard. As I walked out the door, I saw a statue of Saint Joseph and said to him, *My boys need a father; I need your help.* My eyes caught sight of the roses at his feet. Mary had none. There were pink roses at Saint Joseph's feet. I looked up at the huge crucifix over the altar and said to Jesus, *You have to hand it to me in my hand. If you are serious about this I need to know this is of God.*

Later that day, I went to pick up my daughter, who worked for a friend of mine at her daycare center. I was waiting for her in my car and was looking for something in my purse. I felt something next to my window and was startled. It was my friend with a huge bouquet of flowers. Fall flowers—red, yellow, orange, and white. As I took them, I saw it: dead center, in the middle of the bouquet was a pink rose; it did not go at all. I had asked for a yellow rose to stay and a pink one to move. I got the chills and realized that God was serious, this was real. My eyes welled up, and I sat in disbelief. My sister Lila was in the car, she had come for a visit from Biloxi, but I felt I could not tell anyone just yet.

I prayed for the next two weeks, asking God all sorts of questions and telling him of my concerns. He answered all my questions and erased all my concerns. Once, as I was leaving daily Mass, an elderly man stopped by the van to say hi and asked how things were going. At one point, he said, "Can you believe they read the wrong reading?"

I couldn't believe what I heard—one of my concerns was answered in that reading. In talking with people randomly, they would say something that had something to do with a question I had asked God about. When I went back to my spiritual director two weeks later, and I told him the story, his reply was, "Sounds like God wants you to go to New Jersey." His only advice was to not to sell the house for two years.

I continued to pray about it, and by the end of January I had made the decision to tell everyone about the move. We moved in May of 2000. To pack up a twenty-year accumulation of marriage and ten years in that home, and purge what we didn't absolutely need, was an incredible undertaking to say the least—not to mention the twenty-six-foot sailboat, a smaller sail fish boat, a camper, and tons of building tools. We downsized from six bedrooms, four baths, two living rooms, a formal dining room, a big eat-in kitchen, a huge laundry room with play area, a three-car garage, and a shed to a little Cape Cod cottage —two bedrooms with a loft for the girls and one bathroom.

As I was discerning this move, toward the end, I experienced God waiting for me to go forward and to trust him. When I finally made the decision to move, an incredible peace came over me. God did amazing things during that time. His grace was very powerful. Doors opened left and right. Family was supportive, knowing it was God's will, yet they felt the normal sadness.

CHAPTER 31

MOVE NORTH

I went to New Jersey in March to find a place, and God's plan was awesome. It snowed that night, just enough to be beautiful, and the house practically fell in my lap. The church down the street was Saint Therese of the Little Flower, the saint I had prayed to about moving.

We were in New Jersey for ten years. It was God's plan. Not always the easiest because life is a bed of roses—those roses have thorns even when they are intoxicating to smell. To me, that sort of summed up life in New Jersey. The good and the bad; God allows all. In scripture, the book of Job says, "God giveth and God taketh away." After Dav's death, I would open to scripture and many times it would be in the book of Job. At one point, I would whine, "Oh no, Lord, not Job again." I did get to a point where I wanted to learn what God wanted to teach me through that particular book of Job.

I believe it is to keep my eyes on God and have a grateful heart. My spiritual life soared in New Jersey.

We adjusted to the move. Our first summer was nice; you really didn't need air conditioning much up north. That helped with not desiring the beach as it was not really warm enough for me. The fall was incredible with all the colors—breathtaking views for the eyes to behold. Then we came to winter up north. Josh loved it. I remember looking out my kitchen window at the snow and pretending it was the white, sandy beaches of Florida. I had to admit it was beautiful, but driving in it was scary, and slipping on ice was no fun. That happened a few times, but God protected me. It would have helped if there had been a garage. Scraping the car windows and shoveling the driveway were intense workouts for everyone in the house. At times, I did not want to deal with the arguing and whining about scraping the van windows; I would just do it myself. That, in itself, had me looking at my attitude. It needed adjusting. I had to continue asking God to help me have a joyful heart, offering this up to him. I spent many hours in prayer. I was very needy.

I noticed something different at the church we started attending. We were used to hanging around after Mass, chatting with everyone. That did not happen here. The church community had felt overwhelmed by the large number of people from the People of Hope community joining their parish. The parish began to experience being taken over by the People of Hope.

Little did I know, there had been a great persecution against the People of Hope community, which had started at Little Flower church. There I was, in the middle of that persecution. When I asked someone from the People of Hope why no one hung around to chat, I was told that the People of Hope were asked not to, so as to not make the church community feel awkward.

At one point, I found out that I could not be a Eucharistic Minister because I was associated with the People of Hope. That was very hurtful for me. I had always been very involved with our parish. My husband's brother was a priest in Mississippi. I was allowed to become part of the bereavement group, which helped with the funeral masses. I could only be a reader though, not a Eucharistic minister.

At one particular Mass, they did not have enough Eucharistic ministers, and the priest said I would have to step in.

A parishioner said to the priest, in front of me, "She can't."

The priest overruled him, saying that when there was a need, and there was one, I had to be a minister.

That was the most awkward Mass I have ever been part of. I felt like dirt, like nothing. I had the opportunity to embrace the cross, knowing Jesus had been treated more cruelly than I.

The girls had asked the priest on a couple of occasions to come to a function they were part of at school. But the pastor had to decline, because he was under the bishop's authority to not associate with the People of Hope. I experienced pain after pain to my already wounded heart. I knew that I had to continue offering it up, and God would comfort me and he did.

Not long after we moved to New Jersey, I was reading over my past journals, to see where God was leading me. I came to a section where I had said a prayer to Dav to send me wildflowers as a sign he was in heaven. I couldn't remember if I had gotten any flowers, so I reprayed the prayer. One day, not long after that, we went to an outdoor mass for Mary Mother of Hope. Afterward, when I was leaving, I yelled to the kids, "Let's go Arguelles'." I was walking away when Josh, who was five, ran up from behind me and presented me with a handful of wildflowers, saying, "These are for you, these are for you."

What joy I experienced at that moment. I remembered that they were from Dav, but I had to go home and reread the journal entry to remember what they were for. All our married life I would say to Dav, "Just bring me home some wildflowers, don't spend money. It will mean more to me." He really never did it, but he had Josh bring them to me, and for a few years, Josh tended to sporadically bring me flowers from outside.

Adjusting to the north and the fast pace of life in New Jersey was a challenge. Not to mention, the summers were not really summers to me. You could not work in the flower garden until after March 15; down south I usually had flowers blooming by March. The kids could swim in the pool as early as March and continue until November. On occasion, they swam in December too. Going to the beach was great in September, October, and November, and we would be getting to go back as early as April. Not necessarily to swim but to explore and play and have picnics.

That first summer we only went to the beach a couple of times; it was an hour away. Who wanted to drive that far, when I was used to it being ten minutes away?

The first time at the beach with another family was when Josh was about five, and we lost him. When the lifeguard asked what color bathing suit he had on, I did not know. Josh had five of them. After what seemed a long time, one of the other kids found him along the water's edge, down a ways. The beach was covered with people, which was another thing I was not used to. In Pensacola, you could be almost by yourself at the beach, there were so many places to choose from.

One fall, I went on two retreats, one weekend after the other. The first retreat was with our parish; it was a small group of about thirty-five women. What I experienced was God opening my heart about all the pain in my life. That retreat opened a door in my heart for the next retreat, which was the following weekend.

That retreat was with the People of Hope, a much larger group of about 120 women, which was charismatic. Friday night was adoration; that was wonderful. I cried out to God about how angry I was about a lot of things. I had felt duped by God; I believed I had heard him say I was going to get remarried years ago and this had been confusing to me all these years. I had to struggle with that thought and kept giving it to God so as to not let it control me. I needed to stay focused on what was in front of me and on what I needed to be doing at the moment, which always led me back to God's perfect plan and time. That was where I needed to be to keep my peace. In my crying out to God, I ended with "Lord, I have no one to go to, you are all I have. I need you. Help me to get rid of all these feelings. I just want to do your will. Show me your will."

On Saturday night, we had Adoration again, this time with prayer teams of women. They suggested when we were before the Lord to ask him what we should be prayed over for. So I did, I got in line, immediately thinking who do I want to go to. I had my mind on one team, but God had another in mind. I know it will take a lifetime of surrendering my will to God. I trust he is in charge. I told them I had three things that I needed to be prayed over for. I felt like Therese of Little Flower: she wanted it all.

First, I had lost my joy for doing God's will, and I wanted my joy back. Knowing myself, I would continue doing God's will no matter what, but I wanted the joy of the Lord again. Second, I wanted to be healed of all the rejection and pain I had experienced since I had moved there, whether real or not. Third, I shared how I felt, that God had duped me.

The sisters started praying. At one point, one woman said, "I see a vision, God wants you to give him something, physically give him something." She said, "I don't know if it is a little thing or a big thing."

Then another woman said she confirmed that, and she said, "God wants you to literally come and be in Jesus's sacred heart."

The time ended, and I went back to my seat. I realized I hadn't gone up to the altar for Adoration. But for those few minutes, I was still questioning, *What do you want me to give you Lord?*

As I approached the altar, there are only two people there. When I had gone to get prayed over, the whole altar was filled. For me, it was wonderful that there were fewer people. As I placed my face in the veil, I began to start to cry very gently. It felt like a cleansing cry. I was still wondering, *What do you want, God? I can't give it to you unless I know.*

Then I heard a gentle whisper, "Give me David."

I knew then. I saw myself reach deep down in my being, and I pulled a box up that had been wrapped tightly with a chain and lock. I handed it to God. As I was crying, my body began to shake.

The woman next to me put her arm around me and held me, and I heard her saying, "Jesus, Jesus," over and over.

Then I heard, "Give me Danny." This was such a hard one. I had so much pain locked up inside. I saw myself reach down and pull out another box that had been chained and locked up tight; I handed it to him. I had not cried much for Danny, because I had had more of an experience of relief when he died. His agonizing suffering was no more. I had never allowed myself to dwell on the deep pain of his suffering while he was alive. I had to be outwardly strong. I look at it now as a mother's silent, suffering, heart of pain, like Mary our Mother. When I gave God the box, a peace came down upon me from my head to the depths of my being, and my crying stopped very naturally and peacefully. I did not have to get control of myself as I had felt I had to in the past when I started crying.

But God revealed something to me. Four years before, at camp, the girls and women were in the chapel praying. Most everyone was gone and I was before the tabernacle and I had started to cry very hard. A couple of women came and placed their hands on me and began praying. But the words of the prayer made me feel like I was too much for them; I needed to get control of myself. I felt they did not know what to do for me. So at that moment, I used every ounce of determination I had and took that pain and boxed it up tight and wrapped a chain around and around it and put locks on it and stuffed it deep inside. But when I experienced the sister putting her arm around me this time and praying "Jesus, Jesus," I realized all I wanted back then was for someone to hold me and let me cry. God be praised, I was free. I was not finished with life experiences though. We keep going, and we must laugh much.

Another growing in holiness for me was being part of a community, the People of Hope, which I saw as mostly whole families. My thinking was that we were not whole. I had had very strong whole-family relationships when I left Florida. But I realized that forming relationships with couples does not work well if there is no couple. My dilemma was that we were still a family.

Even within the church family, forming family relationships was very difficult. I had a friend tell me, "I wish we had seen you as needy, but you seemed like you had everything under control." I came into the community with the mindset that I would not be a burden on anyone, which created great loneliness. Yet I knew if I was in dire need, I would have had a hundred-plus families helping me. I did meet some wonderful holy people.

Yet God had other plans; each time I experienced loneliness, I gave it to him, and he loved me through it. Trusting that God was about a work in me. I had to rejoice in some of the life lessons he taught me.

One in particular was how God gave me the children as gifts, yet during their growing years, I did not always see it that way. Now that the dust has settled, I see how everything that happened was my training for life—not this life on earth, but my eternal life. My eternal life with God that will never end, and I will have no more pain or sorrow, only joy! No matter what he gives me today, or whatever comes, I know he will always be with me if I only allow him in my heart, and I can experience great joy and peace in the midst of what life brings. It's the hope—hope beyond what we cannot see or feel or hear ; hope that no one or nothing can take from you; hope that goes beyond this life of suffering, to enjoy the good this life has for us.

For a time, I was afraid of enjoying anything good from life. I was waiting for that other shoe to drop. I wanted to make sure I was ready for another suffering. Well, who's in control? I wanted to make sure I was not surprised. If you live like that, you don't allow yourself to be surprised with the good things God has for you either. Getting beyond that fear, which was not of God, took prayer and others supporting me spiritually. When the fear is gone, there is no need to feel you need to be in control. When an emotion surfaces, most of the time I need to check: where is this really coming from? Life is hills and valleys never ending, like laundry and dishes are never ending. This is where we need the joy of the Lord, in our every day to day lives.

The last few years in New Jersey, God placed a recently widowed friend in my path. Her name was Ginny. It was winter, and I decided to bring her homemade potato soup and hot beer bread. She introduced me to Scrabble which I found I enjoyed and then we discovered traveling was fun too.

Our first trip was to New York City, where her son got us a hotel room. She needed to get away. We visited a few churches and museums. We enjoyed dining out, and we realized both of us enjoyed chocolates—a lot.

One day after playing Scrabble, I asked her, "Where would you like to go on our next adventure."

She said, without hesitation, "Rome, for the beatification of Mother Teresa."

I excitedly said, "Let's go."

The trip was incredible, God blessed us abundantly. We even got to go to Assisi; we both love the life of Saint Francis.

We went to Canada for the Eucharistic Congress, which was an exciting incredible experience.

Ginny's son was doing missionary work in Honduras. We got to go during Holy Week for ten days. A whole new world was shown to us. I remember thinking, *This is so hard on the flesh, yet my spirit is soaring.* Serving the people was a gift. They had nothing, and they were joyful and spirit filled.

Greece and a cruise for a few days was our last trip. That pilgrimage was in the footsteps of Saint Paul. We followed his path and visited many of the places he preached. I learned so much, and the scriptures have never been the same when I read of those different areas.

Ginny was a blessing for me and she loved my children. We discovered Cape May the shore at the tip of New Jersey. Wonderful memories. Many times we felt our husbands' intervention.

CHAPTER 32

VACATIONS DOWN SOUTH

We had moved to New Jersey in 2000 and the following summer of 2001, I decided we would go to Biloxi to visit for the first two weeks of June. I made the plane reservations and then realized I was going to have to take the kids out of school a week and a half early. Down south, the kids would have already been out for summer break. Up north, school started later and ended later. The plans were made, and we went.

As soon as we landed, I received a call that they had found my dad in his bed; he had hemorrhaged, and he had been there a few days. For me, the amazing thing was that he had had a rosary in his hand. The last conversation I had with my father on the phone was a few weeks before his death. I had mentioned something about my mother, and I must have hit a nerve; he got upset, going on and on. I just responded with repeated apologies; that was not what I had intended. He finally said, "It's okay. When I get upset, I just say my rosary, and I get back my peace." God had me hear this so I would have a peace about him being alone when he died. He had his rosary in his hand. God had me there for the services, which was a blessing. An African woman who lived next door to him wanted to say a few words about him. As a child, I remembered that my father was prejudiced. I wondered what this woman was going to say. She talked about how he would talk with her and that he was always so kind. God had done an amazing thing. My father's heart had softened over the years.

In April of 2002, we went to Biloxi for Easter break. My sisters encouraged me to come sooner rather than waiting till the summer. My mother was very sick. She had emphysema; she had smoked since she was fourteen, although she wished she could have stopped. I made the reservations, and we went. It was so good for my children to be able to spend time with her, one-on-one. I remember one moment in particular from that week. My mother was begging us for more medicine; we had just given her some not an hour before, and we could not give her more for three to four more hours. She was in so much agony and anxiety from not being able to catch her breath. At that point, I said to my mom, "Mom, we can't give you any more medicine. The only thing we can do is pray."

In a very weak voice, she responded, "Then pray, pray."

I did not need any more encouragement. I began to pray charismatically (praying out loud by repeating short phrases, "Praise you, Jesus. Come, Holy Spirit. We love you, Jesus"), and my two sisters who were there followed. That was one of the most blessed moments of my life with my mom and sisters. My mother quietly repeated most of what I said, and she experienced God's grace and became peaceful; she relaxed back in the bed and was able to rest for a while.

The week came to a close, and we had to leave. I felt that the children needed to get back to school. As we were leaving for the airport, my sister called me and said, "Hospice says Mom will die within twenty-four hours." She wanted me to stay. I felt I had to go. I just prayed. She died that night. The next morning my sister called and said, "We want you to come home. Mom had an insurance policy, and I'm buying you a ticket."

I returned home, and it was so good to be with my siblings and not be a mom at that time. We siblings felt we were the old ones with both our parents gone. It was a new chapter in our lives.

The next summer, in 2003, I made our plans to go down south. Josh's godfather had become sick six weeks earlier and died suddenly. They had held the funeral in south Florida and then planned one in Pensacola, which happened to be around the time of our visit. God's plan. The children and I started wondering what was going on. Why were all of these people in our lives dying when we are there for a visit? I came to the conclusion that this was all a gift. God had me get the idea to plan our vacation time so we would be there for these important events in our families' and friends' lives. I would not have spent the extra money to go back down again. Some gifts are hard to accept. God's are always the best though. So I was back to God's plan, which gave me comfort.

In 2004, I planned our visit for Christmas, my father-in-law's health was declining, and my brother-in-law Paul encouraged me to come down. We arrived and had a wonderful day on Christmas with our immediate and extended family. That night, my father-in-law's only sister, Aunt Pat, died in her home. We had just spent the day with her, and she loved my girls. She liked art, and Autumn was very artsy. We cannot believe another family member dies. God be Praised.

In 2005, I went to Biloxi four times. Danah and I went in April for my niece's wedding, my sister Lila's daughter Stephanie. That was a joyful occasion. It was the first trip in five years of visiting with no deaths.

While I was there, I was led to look for a house to buy, mostly as an investment. Once I sold my house in Florida, I felt I needed to reinvest the money. At first, I started looking for a house in New Jersey; I put a bid on four houses, and on each one, someone overbid me at the last minute. When it happened on the last house, I remember going to God and crying out, "What's going on? What do you want me to do?"

I had a thought, *Buy a house in Mississippi, and rent it.*

Man, you should have heard my reply, "Oh no! Lord! I've been there, done that. I don't want to rent out again. Most people don't take care of other people's property."

I had part of a day to look for a house on the day before the wedding. I felt that if God wanted me to buy a house there, he would make it happen. I had a realtor take me around. Right around lunch, my friend Ann, from high school, called. She and her husband met me, and we had lunch together. We ended up going around looking at homes and areas. They brought me to a house they owned and rented out. Across the street was a house for sale. We called the realtor and got to go in within an hour. It was perfect: a garage, three bedrooms, a nice living room, a small kitchen and dining room, and one and a half baths. It was a ranch design, situated on a large lot. The price was almost half of what I had gotten for my house in Florida. I would be able to fix it up. I drew up a design for cabinets and a center island and had someone give me an estimate. I planned to knock out the wall that connected the kitchen and dining room and enlarging the opening of the door to the living room for the spaces to flow better. I was excited. Then, on top of that, my niece Stephanie asked if they could rent the house from me. It was a good fit.

The second visit that year was in June, we went down south as a family for vacation, and I closed on the house I had bought, finished the details of the plans for the kitchen, and set up the cabinet installation.

That June, my father-in-law died, and there we were again. We were really getting nervous, but again, we needed to remind ourselves that it was a blessing to be there during that time. We went back to New Jersey. Camp for the kids was at the end of August, and then school started.

We all go back in July of 2005, for another niece's wedding; she was on the Arguelles's side of the family. Jorrie was also Dav's and my godchild. It was a good time seeing so many relatives.

On August 29, 2005, Hurricane Katrina hit the Gulf Coast, and Biloxi was devastated. Many of our immediate family members and friends lost everything. My sister Kathy and her family had lived with my mom in the house we all grew up in. When they returned home, there was nothing left standing. You could stand in the yard and make a 180-degree turn and see nothing left standing. You could see the beach. Kathy and her family did not leave till the very last minute. The house was half brick. The bricks were lying flat out all around where the house stood. My niece, who had just gotten married in July, returned to nothing. Dav's sister, Teresa had six feet of water. She had to gut the whole house and start over. My sister Lila had four to five feet of water, and they gutted everything too, which they did all by themselves. In the first few weeks, as they were carrying everything out of the house, Lila slipped and broke her wrist. My friend Ann went home to nothing but rubble. It was a horrible situation. The shrimp factories and warehouses of chicken to be shipped out had just scattered over miles, and the stink and contamination were awful.

God blessed me with the house I had just bought. Every house on the street had water but mine and the lady's next door. I would not have gotten any insurance money if I had gotten water inside. A huge tree had fallen on the back of my house, which was where the kitchen was. I had wanted to redo the kitchen anyway. Now I was getting a new roof and money for the damage to the ceilings and kitchen. God be praised.

It wasn't safe to go down south right away. I finally decided to go down for the month of November to get my house in order and to help out some of the family. My fourth visit that year I stayed for the whole month of November, not knowing what to expect, but God had done amazing things in placing the right people in my path to do the jobs needed.

My older brother, Ricky and his son, Derrick came and did many things that month in between all the work they were doing. Many other family members and cousins helped me with all sorts of details. Even Lila, who had a lot on her plate, came a few times to help me. My friend Toni, in Pensacola, came for a few days and helped at Lila's with me. Autumn was an adult now, and she flew down for a few days to help. There were daily miracles; God was in charge.

I had talked to the cabinet guy in September, and he was able to build my kitchen cabinets and have them ready for me when I was there in November. He had it all put together the week before I left. God's perfect plan.

I learned so much that month while I was in Biloxi. Our

whole life is about learning. I believe that's how you have to look at everything that happens to you.

If I think life is a lemon I need to make lemonade. I think the sugar is acts of kindness, thanksgiving, serving others, and just loving.

CHAPTER 33

LOVE IS A DECISION

We are called to love and from that will come pain. So, do we choose to not love? I say no, because not loving is living in isolation, which is far worse.

I have learned that sometimes we give ourselves crosses, which we need to ask forgiveness for in order to experience peace and joy. An example would be, pursuing my own agenda over my responsibilities. My family would suffer. Cranky kids because I didn't go to the store and get milk for cereal. The next morning is chaos. Had I thought of their needs instead of my own wants, the household would have run smoother. I created my own cross.

The crosses God gives us are the ones that have sacrificial redemption when we embrace them. Like my husband's and son's death. God did amazing things for me when I embraced that cross.

I myself can have moments of wanting to hug past crosses and stay there too long. I need to keep moving forward. There is so much more to do in this short life. Yes, I can grow from my crosses and help others in their crosses, but to be paralyzed in fear of what's next, is not where God wants me to be.

I am free because I am loved by God, not because I did anything to deserve it.

So we are back to the word *love*. This word can be meditated on for a lifetime and still never be exhausted. God's love is out of the box. That is my new saying: Get out of the box. I believe we sometimes put God in a box when we can no longer see the miracles that he can do for us. The bigness of God's love for us is beyond our mind's comprehension.

It's 2013, I still experience the pain. Thank God it is not to the same degree.

Taking time with God was critical for my survival. The survival is not as intense now, yet I am still clinging, because I experience such great joy and peace from within. There are still challenges, but they are different. We are not perfect, we just need to be striving for perfection.

We all have a choice to choose Love.

Love is a decision.